Also By Christine Kloser

A DAILY DOSE OF LOVE
Everyday Inspiration to Help You Remember
What Your Heart Already Knows

PEBBLES IN THE POND
Transforming the World One Person at a Time
(Wave One)

PEBBLES IN THE POND
Transforming the World One Person at a Time
(Wave Two)

PEBBLES IN THE POND
Transforming the World One Person at a Time
(Wave Three)

CONSCIOUS ENTREPRENEURS
A Radical New Approach to Purpose, Passion and Profit

THE FREEDOM FORMULA
How to Put Soul in Your Business
and Money in Your Bank

INSPIRATION TO REALIZATION
Real Women Reveal Proven Strategies for Personal,
Business, Financial and Spiritual Fulfillment

PEBBLES

in the

POND

*Transforming the World
One Person at a Time*

~Wave Four~

Transformation Books
York, PA

Pebbles in the Pond: Transforming the World One Person at a Time (Wave Four)

Published by:
Transformation Books
211 Pauline Drive #513
York, PA 17402
www.TransformationBooks.com

ISBN: 978-0-9862901-2-1

Cover design by Sarah Barrie
Layout and typesetting by Ranilo Cabo
Editor: Marlene Oulton, www.MarleneOulton.com
Proofreader: Allison Saia
Printed in the United States of America

Help Me Be...

Strong enough to be vulnerable.

Wise enough to realize how little I know.

Loving enough to embrace my "enemy."

Tender enough to be powerful.

Smart enough to realize I can't do it alone.

Brilliant enough to shine the light of others.

Doubtful enough to know the power of faith.

Courageous enough to share my truth.

~ Christine Kloser

Table of Contents

Introduction

"A small body of determined spirits fired by an unquenchable faith in their mission can alter the course of history."
– Gandhi

THANK YOU FOR FOLLOWING THE WHISPER in your heart to pick up this book and crack open the cover. My guess is – like the contributors to this book – you've been on a powerful, transformational journey that sometimes joyously surprises you and other times throws you an unexpected curve ball that knocks you to your knees.

Perhaps as you read this you're in the middle of the most challenging time of your life. Or maybe you've just come through a difficult situation with a renewed sense of faith and hope. Perhaps you have a niggling sense that a growth opportunity is lurking around the corner waiting for you, but you just don't know what it is... yet.

No matter where you stand right now on your path, I trust that since you're here – taking time to read this book – you believe in the concept of a "pebble in the pond" and share in the vision of a world that is transformed one person at a time.

While world transformation may seem like a far-fetched dream, the truth I've come to know is that as we transform as individuals, we *do* make a difference in the lives of those around us. And if you've ever thrown a stone in a still pond, you know that

1

one single splash sends ripples outward in every direction, creating more and more ripples. It's the same thing when that "splash" is the impact of your life and how you live it each and every day – the impact expands.

It doesn't matter if you're a leading-edge entrepreneur, schoolteacher, mom, rocket scientist, doctor, writer, healer, manager, salesperson, nurse, volunteer, retiree, or anything else; your life – and how you live it – can be a force for good in our world. Every person has the power to make a difference, including you, and that's exactly what this book is about.

At this time in history we are on the precipice of experiencing the new world many people have been dreaming about – a world filled with love, cooperation, contribution, service, community, and abundance for all. And there are a growing number of people who are doing all they can to heal themselves, become a part of the solution (simply by being who they truly and authentically are), and bring more light and love into the world.

In the pages of this book you'll meet such visionary leaders and world-changers. You might recognize some of the contributors as bestselling authors and leading entrepreneurs. Others aren't as well known, yet their stories are testaments to the power of one person's transformational journey to send ripples of good into the world.

I personally feel so blessed to receive the gift of working closely with most of the contributors to this book. We've gathered together over the course of eight months to birth this book in service to you. As you discover each contributor's story, you'll see why I consider it a blessing to call them my clients, soul travelers, and friends. *Pebbles in the Pond – Wave Four* is only possible because of the love and light they bring to the world.

Some chapters will make you cry, while others will make you laugh. Some will touch your heart deeply, while others will inspire you to think differently. Some chapters will be difficult to read as you hear of the challenges a few of the authors have faced that nobody should ever have to live through. And others will offer you a heartfelt reassurance that if they can do it (whatever the "it" is), you can, too.

So as you proceed through this book, don't feel the need to read the chapters in order. Chances are as you peruse the table of contents or randomly flip open the pages, you will receive exactly the message that is meant for you in that moment. Above all else, let the stories in this book bathe you in love, compassion, understanding, and inspiration to transform your challenges and struggles (large or small) into beautiful blessings for yourself and others.

You never know what miracle may happen as a result of reading one of these stories. In fact, this book series in and of itself is evidence of the miraculous grace that appeared during the most challenging time of my life. In the first "wave" of *Pebbles in the Pond* (published in 2012), the title of my chapter was "The Best 'Worst' Time of My Life."

It was the worst time because I was going through personal bankruptcy and a very challenging dissolution of a business partnership, unsure about how I was going to support my family and questioning everything about who I knew myself to be. Saying I felt like a failure puts it mildly. Yet that challenging time opened my heart in ways I never knew possible – and one of the many "gifts in the challenge" was the concept for this book series.

With this – Wave Four of *Pebbles in the Pond* – the ripples continue to encompass and empower you to be who you are here to be… and to let your light shine!

On behalf of myself and all of the contributing authors of this series, we send you our deepest blessings that this book delivers the inspiration and transformation your soul is seeking. May you be guided by grace.

Love and blessings,
Christine Kloser,
Spiritual Guide ~ Award-Winning Author
Transformational Book Coach ~ Publisher

ᕲ

No More Hiding.
No More Playing Small

Christine Kloser

IT HAPPENED IN A MOMENT – the realization that as "big" and wonderful as I thought my life was, I was still playing small and hiding my brightest light. Until that moment I hadn't seen it. I really thought I was living my soul's true purpose, making the contribution I was put on Earth to make, and doing a pretty good job at it. But until this glimpse into a new reality – and a new possibility – I was basically asleep to the full potential of my life and the light I was designed to bring to the world.

Maybe you've felt the same way at times in your life. Everything appears one way one moment and then a sudden realization changes everything and helps you see the illusion you've been living. It reminds me of that Jim Carrey movie, *The Truman Show*. In the movie, Truman's entire life had been lived on a TV set without his knowing it. He thought he was living in a big, beautiful world, experiencing life to the fullest, while millions of people were actually watching him in his own TV reality show that he didn't know existed. As far as he knew life "off the set" didn't exist – until that fateful moment when everything changed and he realized that the "sky" above him was fixed and fake and there was something on the other side, which he became determined to discover.

Now, my moment of realization wasn't nearly as dramatic as Truman's. As some of our most profound moments are, this one was subtle. It came out of a period of time when I'd really been reflecting, questioning, expanding, healing, and growing in my life – re-creating myself in a sense. And almost like the simple act of placing a cherry atop a delicious ice cream sundae, I could simply see a more complete picture.

I saw how the success I had created in my life since going through bankruptcy and foreclosure and losing a business to a former business partner all in the same year was not the full picture of my life and my work. It was just the first step to what I was put here to do.

As I write this, it's interesting to reflect on that moment because while I'm aware that there is so much more expression, so much more life force, so much more of the Divine that wants to be revealed through me, I'm not there… yet. I'm still in the beginning phases of opening to see who I really, truly, Divinely am and fully understanding what God put me here for in the first place.

I want to share a little back story with you to help you understand why this awareness was such a wake-up call for me, and also help you see how there may be a subtle wake-up call happening in your own life.

When I was growing up, I never felt good enough. Like many people, this belief is something I came into this world with to heal and transform as I evolved and remembered who I was. It took me several decades to get to where I am now, with some understanding of the larger, soul-directed purpose of my life.

But when I was younger, I longed to feel important, special, seen, heard, valued, and appreciated for who I was. It wasn't a conscious awareness, but looking back I can see the evidence in my path. Since I wasn't a very good student, I learned to excel by performing: dancing, figure-skating, gymnastics, and majorettes to name a few. They all put me in the limelight and helped me feel good enough, at least temporarily, while I performed and won applause.

Fast-forward to my adult life as an entrepreneur since 1991, and the same cycle continued. I excelled as a yoga teacher at a time when the biggest dream I could imagine was to teach yoga at a studio in Los Angeles owned by Rod Stryker and Steve Ross. That was my big, audacious life goal. It happened and I felt good enough... for a short while. Can you see the pattern of my playing small and hiding begin to emerge? Really? My biggest dream was to teach a yoga class at that studio? Looking back I can see how small I was thinking... and being.

Over seven years I went from being a fitness trainer to teaching yoga to owning my own yoga studio. Then I started a women's networking group in Los Angeles, which led to running events, seminars, and business coaching, and launching a publishing company.

While all of this was exciting, fun, and making a difference to others, under the radar – under my own conscious mind – I was still searching, hoping that maybe "this" next thing would bring me some peace and lasting satisfaction. I couldn't dream beyond what I could see because I was looking for any piece of the validation, acceptance, and accolades I believed I needed. My everyday life was focused on this pursuit rather than on a vision of what I truly wanted for my life. I kept hiding my doubts, hiding my fears, and hiding my light by trying to keep it all together in the hope that people wouldn't see that underneath it all I still didn't feel good enough and couldn't see anything more for myself.

Eventually the unstable foundation I had created internally couldn't sustain what I was attempting to build as my impenetrable fortress of success on the outside and everything I had built came crumbling down at once. I lost my home, my business, all of my money, and almost my marriage in my crash of 2011.

It was by far the most challenging thing I've experienced to date in my life. And it was also the greatest gift, because I couldn't hide anymore. I could no longer keep up the front that I was fine, business was great, and I had my act together. I could no longer hold together the pieces that made me feel good enough. I had no choice but to let go and let it be. Painful as that was, it transformed everything about my life.

I've since built a successful, sustainable, and profitable business helping authors around the world share their wisdom, message, and story on the pages of a book. *Pebbles in the Pond* being in your hands right now is part of that success. To date I've trained more than 70,000 authors around the world, launched a new publishing company, seen many of my clients become bestselling authors, facilitated life-changing live events for global audiences, and more. I have to admit, life is good... really good!

And, in the midst of this beautiful phase of my life, I caught that glimpse of something else – that nudge that says, "You ain't seen nothin' yet"; that voice that says I'm just getting started; that part of me that quite honestly gets terrified at times about where this path is leading me.

I'm beginning to see that the "bigness" of my life and the work I'm blessed to do is only a fraction of what I was put here on Earth to accomplish; that only a small fragment of my brightest light is really being revealed; that I am cautious with, as one of my teachers says, "How much God I'm willing to let others see through me."

As I wrote that sentence, I could feel the immediate urge to delete it out of fear of what you'll think of me – fear that I'd rather play small and keep it safe than open up to my full God-intended expression; that I'd rather hide than risk being attacked or ridiculed when I shine my light fully.

So while I do have this amazing business and life now, believing it's the biggest I can dream is a disservice to my soul. It's a beautiful distraction that can easily keep me from going deeper, surrendering more, and opening up to the Universe in a bigger way. It can make it look like I really am living my soul's highest purpose... until I look closer.

I know in some ways the evolution of the past years was needed and has stretched me and helped me grow and evolve in ways in which I've become unrecognizable to myself. For example, one day, after my husband had heard me say something out of character when we were driving somewhere, he later joked that he thought he had picked up a hitchhiker! I had said something and been with him in a way I never had before. I get it. I have grown and evolved.

After this glimpse of a whole new world I realize that what I've created is likely only the beginning of something outside my current realm of possibility. It's exciting, scary, thrilling, and nerve-wracking all at the same time. And... I wouldn't want it any other way.

After sharing this with you, I want to invite you to reflect on your own life. Honestly assess whether you are playing full-out, sharing your highest expression with the world, and bringing forth the creative expression of your bright, beautiful soul... or not.

You might see immediately that you aren't... yet... which is totally okay. I'm not either, and very few people on the planet are at that stage in their lives. We are all evolving and growing. And if, like me, you didn't see it right away because life is feeling and looking good right now, it may take a little digging to pull back the curtain and assess where you are and whether you're doing and being all that your soul put you here to do and be.

One thing I know to be true on this journey is that we are all, in our unique ways, here to live an amazing life, experience joy, make a difference, and feel fulfilled on a deep, soul level. Playing small and hiding – especially when it looks to the world like you aren't – doesn't serve you or anyone on this journey.

The question is... are you willing to join me? Are you willing to catch a glimpse of a new possibility for your life that's far beyond anything you can envision in your mind right now? You don't need to have any idea what it is; you only need to be *willing*, and open your heart and soul for more to be revealed. It's the willingness that makes the difference.

9

Here are a few affirmations to help you move forward on your path of no more hiding and no more playing small:

- I am willing to see a new possibility for my life.
- I am safe to go on this journey.
- I am a cherished and deeply loved child of the Universe.
- I am here to do all I was put here to do.
- I am here to experience and BE the light of my soul.

It's time to step into your own greatness and see how truly wonderful life can be!

Christine Kloser, "The Transformation Catalyst," is a spiritual guide, award-winning author, and transformational book coach whose spot-on guidance transforms the lives of visionary entrepreneurs and authors around the world. Her coaching and training programs have impacted more than 70,000 authors to help them unleash their authentic voices and share their messages on the pages of a book. If you have a book inside of you and want help getting it out, get started with Christine's FREE video training here: www.GetYourBookDone.com/webinar.

Dancing Home into the House that Love Built

Nancy Baker

I COULD GUESS THAT A HIGH PERCENTAGE of people would think my life was extremely boring, and more than a handful might deem it mind-numbingly dull. As a creative artist I have the blessing of filling my schedule with large expanses of alone time, enjoying quiet and solitude, spending endless hours creating art, learning, reading, and thinking. It isn't unusual to begin my day when the sun is coming up, meditating, reading, thinking, writing, creating, pondering, and then notice the sun is going down. Some days I am thankful for the recorded telemarketer calls letting me know the rest of the world still exists.

I appreciate my solitude time knowing it was this precious gift that allowed me to learn how to consciously create my future.

Growing up, my family never talked about dying, or living for that matter. I went to church, but there wasn't spiritual conversation happening there either. Church was something that came with attendance and activities, where one was restricted, regulated, and reigned in to acceptable behavior. Overall there was a lot of pressure to behave and act properly in order to feel approved of.

In my school years I was an average student – above average in a few subjects and below average in others. Yet teachers always liked me because I was shy to comatose, quiet, and fear-filled to always obey. I knew the consequences of someone being unhappy with me so I always wanted to please. I sought approval – not so I could move forward but so I wouldn't be noticed. I wanted to be more than a wallflower in the corner; I wanted to be invisible. I learned to strive for average, normal, indistinguishable, plain, so the attention would never be on me. I could observe life while being invisible – *strive for invisibility* became my unconscious motto.

I developed a sarcastic humor – a default mode I used to avert attention from me. I learned to *listen to respond* rather than *listen to understand*. In a group I'd toss out jokes at any sign of tension. I believed that if I could go along in life and lighten someone's burden for a moment or a day, the world would be a better place because we'd all get along more easily; we'd find a gentler way to live our existence and carry our burdens in a more tolerable way. And this expectation from life – tolerable existence – should be good enough.

For many years this worked for me. I had accepted the fact that this was how I was supposed to live life: carrying burdens, tolerating circumstances, enjoying a few happy moments interspersed with hard work days, making my way through a routine list of things to do, satisfyingly burning the candle at both ends, always putting others' needs before mine. After a good day I slept well, and after a bad day sleep was restless.

Life happens. Things change. Opportunities to ask big life questions showed up for me in a gift, wrapped in divorce papers. Being in the new place of alone-ness with three kids, I unwrapped the luxurious gift of control of the TV remote. Turning it off, I relished the sound of silence for the first time in my life, and I listened to the sounds of my inner me.

12

And I heard:

If I could just stop being so afraid of change, I could reconcile wanting things to be different and wanting things to stay the same.

If I could just have more money, more energy, more month, I could relax for a moment and stop being so hard on myself.

If I could just have one person who could love and understand me for who I am, I'd feel "enough," and willingly change myself to be whatever they wanted me to be.

If I could just find happiness for an hour, I could coast on that feeling for a while longer.

If I could just find another distraction, I could forget how disillusioned I feel.

I started looking for insights into why my life was the way it was, why I had repeatedly made stupid choices, and why there were so many triggers that made me cry. Perhaps if I could find out why I struggled so much, my life would stop feeling so draining.

As I learned to understand how screwy my thoughts were, how crossed my wires had become, I started paying attention to my inner voice who was guiding me to understanding a new way of being, a new way of living. I was compiling a sort of "CliffsNotes" version of what worked for me, and understanding that I could adopt new perspectives. I created effective ways to delete thought programs that were no longer beneficial and replace them with Source's definition and perspective. I discovered my inner essence, my divine connection. I could feel it taking form, integrating into my life, and it became a dance.

I trusted my self. I believed I could learn divine connection with my inner being and I could live from there. Step in. Step out. Step back in. Do the Hokey Pokey dance as you turn your life around. That's what connection is all about. It takes some time before the Hokey-Pokey awkward balancing dance of divine connection becomes

13

smooth. It takes a while before it becomes this beautiful waltz of life and we can dance like Ginger Rogers and Fred Astaire in our divine, magnificent ballroom.

At the beginning, divine connection feels like a childhood game. Then, with willingness and commitment, it becomes like a wedding-reception dance – funny-feeling, a bit exciting, and still off balance. Watching how others do the connection dance, and then feeling the practice of individuality and acceptance, you lose your hold on what others might think. Taking a brave step forward into the big circle, you hear your divine higher self lovingly singing to you some familiar lyrics of an Elvis Presley song: *"Take my hand. Take my whole life too. 'Cause I can't help falling in love with you."*

Accept. Grasp your hand and fall into rhythm, into sync, into love with your divine Magnificent Energy, with your truest self. Let yourself feel held by the loving arms of your inner Source, waltzing in bare feet to the orchestrations of angels, knowing life is all good. Knowing life is all divine. Knowing life is all *magnificent!* Respond to your inner calling, accept the invitation to dance, and proclaim, *"Yes! I am ready! I know it is time for me to come home!"*

It is time to come home. Home to your birth-light, to your inner space, to your inner Grace of divine union with your spiritual self. You've been gone too long. It is time to feel welcomed home into your inner place of self-love where you are held in the loving arms of acceptance, approval, understanding, and compassion, feeling and knowing that Source just can't help but fall in love with *you!*

You are being called home to your inner essence that is yearning to be host for your divine partnership; yearning to teach you to build a home with a solid foundation of unconditional love permeated with acceptance, approval, and inward lightness, as your place to own, to live in, to commune with daily – a home built on a solid foundation where divine orchestrations abound.

Your higher self is patiently waiting to teach you to create your birth-light home where you are safe – safe to create your life in ways that allow you to embrace your thoughts, feel your emotions, and be free from judgment and seeking approval. Home where you learn to hear your inner voice clearly confirming that you are free, loved, understood – free to feel your passion, loved into fearlessly embracing your purpose, understood divinely and intimately while you dialogue with Source, revealing your unique life and mission. Home with your confident self, recognizing the inner voices of thought that are no longer beneficial – thoughts that hold you back from willingly releasing your outdated programming to angelic guidance for loving transformation into Source's perspective.

Now is the time to build your new home, constructed of new materials gifted to you by Source, and transform your thinking and habits. Now is your time to let loose and let love become you. Let love uncover you, and discover your birth-light to bridge the gap between your heart and your higher divine self. It is time to shine your divine light, accepting and embracing being called home to dance with your divine self-love, knowing Source deeply loves, approves, and accepts all of you, today, just as you are. It is time to embody your essence and live in your divine, love-built home.

Everyone has a divine spiritual essence – a love-built home, a place of divine connection to our birth-light that is the well of Magnificent Energy within us. How effectively we choose to use this connection is our personal choice.

Allowing outdated, ineffective habits and stagnant beliefs to guide us can cause life to feel off balance. We were born into this lifetime on the extension of generational lines of people who effectively learned, demonstrated, and taught us to shut down emotions as a means of ease of survival and a mode to eliminate pain, alleviate suffering, and diminish heartache. Shutting down emotions and feeling less is a coping mechanism, a default mode; it is something to do when we don't know any other way or path to home.

However, building a loving, mutually beneficial, two-way connection with divine essence creates a feeling place, a feeling space of energy to fuel our thoughts in support of our life and dreams. Learning effective ways to self-love, self-tend, and self-care allows divine truth to reveal our source of appreciation, and creates a supportive connection to thrive and flourish. Learning the benefits of our divine essence and clearing the obstacles in our path to hosting clear, cooperative connection allows us to move forward into a future of emotional engagement in beneficial, uplifting ways that create loving foundations for all relationships – casual, intimate, and spiritual.

When you tend self and build your divine relationship as your foundation, you are free to engage with others on a higher level, offering the best you have to gift to others as acceptance, approval, and seeing them as full of potential and possibility. This is the foundation that changes the world, that lets loose and lets love uncover true resources to fully allow experiencing divine life.

You are the common denominator in all of your life experiences; it is up to you to hear and respond to the calling from your inner soul to live in a new experience of self. It takes courage to open to new innovative perspectives and allow Source to assist you in creating a workable definition of connection that fully benefits your life experience. It takes willingness to shine light on the awareness of where you are in your life journey and to believe in what your life can become. Learning, understanding, and implementing tools and daily practices are key steps to uncovering the power of your Magnificent Energy and opening to a life guided by joy and unconditional love.

Take the first step towards your divine love-built home. Ask Source: *What will that life FEEL like for me?* Then feel your emotions created by embracing the empowering words below, gifted to you by Source, and embark on the divinely supportive relationship that awaits you.

- I recognize my partnership with Source is answering my prayers.
- I know that out of these changes only good will come.

16

- I appreciate trusting faith and taking actions feeling comfortably natural to me.
- I feel and know I am proud of my Self as I visualize improving me.
- My life improves in dynamic and much-needed ways.
- I am on course for miracles in the ways I plan and take action.
- I am choosing powerful belief in trusting my Self to learn to fully love me all ways!

Divine Relationship Expert, **Nancy Baker,** helps individuals who are tired of seeking approval, feeling judged, and are ready to comprehensively understand divine connection and implement effective daily practices encouraging self-love, self-tend, and self-care. She is the author of *Looking for Love in All the Right Places* and founder of Self Love University. Begin your transformation with "I Love Me! Notes" at SelfLoveUni.com, and proclaim, *"Yes! I am ready to dance home into the house that love built!"*

Bad Little Good Girl and The Lovely Painting!

Stephanie Bavaro

"GOD NEVER GIVES US MORE THAN WE CAN HANDLE!" Okay, I can accept that, but did God have to trust me so much this year?

Like the star in a bad made-for-TV movie, I endured betrayal, massive financial loss, forgery, attack, denial, and a lingering lawsuit... all at the hands of two family members (bless them). I also initiated and then had to grieve the final ending to a precious but challenging five-year relationship. Sure, there was joy, too: My 2013 telesummit, GREATful Woman™ Talks!, reached thousands and birthed a string of successful GREATful Woman products and services, including my first book, a #1 international bestseller.

I'd like to tell you that I balanced the year's events with gratitude, but let's start with complete transparency. I retreated into a four-month blur of semi-isolation and overdosing on Netflix in an opossum-like survival mode — like if I didn't move, nothing else could hurt me. Here I was, a GREATful Woman, beacon of gratitude and abundance, brought to my emotional, spiritual, and physical knees. I was down, but I was far from out! With a violated bank account, bruised ego, fragile heart, and slightly desecrated spirit, I finally surrendered and asked for help. It was from this weakest point that I found my courage, strength, and desire to live — not just to exist anymore. From our depths can come radical healing and growth, if we allow it... and if we do the work. Thank heaven I did and I am.

Let's start with one life-altering "aha": My life had been ruled by my being the "good little girl" — the loving daughter, friend, sister, employee, and girlfriend. I too often did what people asked of me without ensuring it was in *my* best interest to (or first). It became painfully clear that I was the "*bad* little good girl," paying the toxic cost of always doing the right thing for everyone else. This past year alone, my Good Girl decisions cost me money, esteem, family, trust, relationships, health, and a lovely painting.

And this is where our story really begins... with a lovely painting.

Salvatore and I had met (about five years ago) when he was our chauffeur on the first day of a thirteen-person, eight-day tour of Italy's Amalfi Coast. Our love was sweet, genuine, and deep. Romantic, right? At times it was. Our love itself was a beautiful gift, and our challenge was manifesting that love in a relationship that met both our needs. We were together on and off for those five years. I'm GREATful that in the end my stubbornness to hold a place of love, light, and possibility for us lost out to his stubbornness to meet his familial obligations from his comfort zone. Despite my Good Girl attempts to ignore my own needs, I was set free to love and be loved wholeheartedly.

Salvatore and I were complete (*break-up* is such a misnomer) in the beginning of October. Three weeks later I was told that he'd agreed to marry *(WHAT?!)* a local woman he'd recently met who would help him with his familial obligations *(THE?!)*, and the wedding would be in December *(BLEEP?!)*. In truth, I felt a strange mixture of pure relief and deep grief — relief that I no longer needed to hold a space of light and love for him and relief that I no longer had to consider shrinking to fit inside his comfort zone, all while genuinely grieving the loss of this important man and friendship from my life.

I spent Thanksgiving in Florence with a dear friend, Elizabeth, a fabulous American who's lived in Italy for twenty-five years and who had introduced Salvatore to me. While visiting her, I mentioned that I was sad about "losing" a gorgeous painting that I had commissioned of the US Capitol Building; it was for the home that Salvatore and I would have shared in Italy together. I'd left the painting in Amalfi when I needed to go to America for Christmas the previous year, fully expecting to return three months later more permanently. Little did I know that would be the last time Salvatore and I would see each other, and that we would end our relationship eight months after that. Should I have to lose my painting just because he physically had it? Elizabeth offered to send Salvatore a simple text to courier the painting up to Florence.

He texted back (in Italian, of course) that Elizabeth was the only person who understood what he WANTED in his life versus what he MUST DO for his family. He was hoping to keep the painting and hang it, but if she thought it was best to return it, he would. From this unexpected response, I slumped down in the corner of this year's boxing ring and cried. There was no winner. I cried for all I had lost this year, including my best friend. I cried for all that would be and all that never would.

I threw up my hands and said, "Screw it! Let him have it! I don't care."

Then I just froze. I paused as a cosmic light bulb ignited.

"Wait! That's the old me. That's the Bad Little Good Girl in me who contributed in some ways to everything that happened this year. The old me, the Good Girl, would just let him have it. But what is the *loving* thing for me to do?"

I didn't know. "I need some time to think about this. It's not about the painting. It's about my learning a new language. It's about making the most loving choice for my higher self."

I prayed, meditated, and consulted two of my coaches. Interestingly, the most poignant message came from an unexpected (and entertaining) source. Elizabeth has a friend, Luciana, who reads Tarot cards. Fun! Luciana is a fabulous, eccentric, Florentine woman who lives in a top-floor apartment that is a whirlwind of clutter and cats and energy. She has this wild, long, gray hair that she constantly pulls up and back and out, like maneuvering antennae to help her mind tune in.

It's no coincidence that we were scheduled to see Luciana on the same day that we received the text. So I asked her what I should do about the painting. She dealt the cards, stopped, and looked intently at me. She slowly and deliberately said (in Italian),

"You must...

Listen to me...

You must...

Get That Painting Back!"

Huh? Elizabeth and I just looked at each other with our jaws on the table. Then Luciana said the words I'll never forget, words that changed and illuminated a chapter of my life... and of my next book. She said, "You've had an unreasonable amount taken from you this year. Your ability to face it all with such grace is a testament to how evolved you are. It's time for you to *start reclaiming what is yours!*"

That may have been the most beautiful compliment I've ever received, but more important, I heard her: It's time for me to start reclaiming what's mine. I think about all I have lost this year – not just the external things like money and relationships, but I lost (as in temporarily misplaced) small pieces of my soul and my heart's true north. It's time to take action to reclaim and mend. My Good Girl is going to have to relinquish the reins.

Pulling up my big-girl panties, a simple text was sent: "Please send the painting." Sure, it seemed from his response (and lack of response) that this would make him angry and/or sad. The truth is that I can't know how he feels and that his reaction has nothing to do with me. One blessing is that I felt no assumption of or responsibility for his reaction. This was not an act of spite or hatred; it was not an act against anyone. It was a loving act towards me. Woo hoo!

22

The painting came in a tube that was too large to fit in my suitcase, so I had to carry it, by hand, from Florence to London and home to McLean, Virginia – on taxis, subways, and planes. I'm fully aware of the significance of this repetitive and uncomfortable manual action. Like any new skill or language, we must consciously practice small repetitive behaviors to form a habit.

When I got home, it was time for me to look at the painting. Salvatore and I had never seen the painting together, so it had never been "ours." It was in the original sealed tube; it was mine. I cleared the dining room table, unpacked the painting, and grabbed a box of tissues. There also was a lush Pinot Noir on call. I was ready.

I carefully cut open the tube. I unrolled the painting and looked at it. Then I had my niece hold it as I walked across the room and really took it in. I won't lie; I expected to cry. A part of me was scared that I'd look at this painting and think of Salvatore and the home that we would never share. But I'd hoped that I'd look at that painting and see that powerful choice to reclaim what was mine. With a peaceful smile, I said, "Wow, that's really colorful. I'm not sure I'd ever hang that up."

The authentic lack of emotional response when I saw that painting told me that I was free. This was not denial. That painting had no hold on me. The memories surrounding that painting had no hold on me. I exhaled five years of loving expectations, confident now that one day the grief I was feeling would have no hold on me.

Can I get a little Amen?

Today I'm exploring this journey in my next book, *Bad Little Good Girl – Healing the Toxic Cost of Always Doing the "Right" Thing!* (Well, that's the working title.) And you know there's a chapter in it entitled "Reclaiming What Is Yours!" It is amazing how many women have proclaimed themselves Bad Little Good Girls to me in the last few months.

What about you? To my women readers, I ask, "Are you a Good Girl – whether it's since you were a child or triggered by an event or relationship? If so, please understand that being the Good Girl comes at a cost. What price have you paid? Money? Time? Love? Health? Self-care? Have you tried to shrink yourself to fit into someone else's world? Or worst of all, have you ever dimmed your light (that which makes you shine) to make others comfortable?

The truth is that we all are *neither* good nor bad... AND we are *both* good and bad. Until we embrace that dichotomy, we'll continue to pay! Feel comfort knowing your Bad Little Good Girl can peacefully retire through a loving process of understanding how she manifests in your life, actively releasing her, and creating a new language and playbook!

This past year, I paid for over forty years of dutiful living as a Bad Little Good Girl! Now I understand and accept that I had to be taken to that depth to wake up. My only responsibility now is to do everything I can to heal, learn, and share my truth. I know that if I don't embrace this Bad Little Good Girl journey, I'm doomed to repeat the costs until I learn or die.

I choose to learn! I choose to heal! And yes, I choose to reclaim what is mine... and it all started with a lovely painting.

As a postscript to this story, a dear friend of mine adores that painting. She thoughtfully waited until she knew how I felt about it before she made a generous offer to purchase. It is now hers. I don't feel that painting was ever mine (or ours). It was just a tool to help me as I started to speak this new language of healthy self-priority and love. It was one of my first active steps out of my Bad Little Good Girl and into my true self, a GREATful Woman!

Stephanie Bavaro, CEO of GREATful Woman™, provides her clients with the clarity, tools, and community to take the next best step towards confidence, joy, and success – on their terms. An award-winning entrepreneur and certified Project Management Professional (PMP), Stephanie offers business consultancy, training (including TeleSummit Success™), transformational interviews with GREATful Woman Talks!, bling with GREATful Gear™, and is a #1 international bestselling author of multiple books. To learn more, please visit www.GREATfulWoman.com.

From Fear to Love:
Receiving Gifts from Life

Sally Bendersky

Survival

IN 1986 I WAS THE SINGLE MOTHER OF A GIRL and a boy who were entering into adolescence. All of us were born and raised in Santiago, Chile. My daughter was fourteen and my son was two years younger. I had been a single parent since their dad and I had separated, when my daughter and son were three and one respectively. I had always dreamed of having four children, but I ended up accepting that it would not happen.

During those years my first priority was to bring home enough money for nurturing, raising, and educating my children. My ex-husband and I had settled on how to distribute the costs and investments that our children would need from us, yet, as in so many broken marriages, he was not consistent in fulfilling his verbal promise. I would never have taken any sort of legal action, since he was always a loving father, especially to our daughter. (I have observed that little babies are frequently not very interesting to their fathers and grandfathers. Our boy was a baby when his father left our home, whereas our daughter was a beautiful and talkative three-year-old little lady.)

27

I had been jobless several times before 1986. I know I had been chosen as the best candidate for some of the jobs that I had applied for, but I was not given them. My interpretation is that many companies were not willing to hire women engineers at that time. It was when I was at home that my children were happiest, because they had my attention whenever they wanted it. I acknowledge that I also immensely loved being closer to them than when I was working, but I also felt lost and confused. I had daily fantasies of suffering deep economic misery, and my sense of self-value was nil.

In the years before and after 1986, nothing could have been further from my thoughts than becoming an entrepreneur. Simply put, it was not an existing option and nobody had ever mentioned such a crazy thing to me. Engineers were taught that our role was to create and maintain the infrastructure for the development of the country. Only intellectually deprived dropouts from rich families went into business. You just had to graduate from your university studies and you would easily have a safe, reasonably well-paying job where you could stay during all your working life. You would either climb the corporate ladder or stay comfortably where you were, earning your salary.

The safe-job illusion crashed in one single day in 1973, when our own Chilean "Tuesday 9/11" took place in the form of a military coup in which the four heads of each branch of the armed forces and police replaced a stormy democratic government and the traditional Parliament, creating a military junta. Half of the country was happy; I belonged to the other half.

My parents tried to convince me that the military coup was just what our country needed. I was still married and our daughter was eighteen months old. In two or three years Chile became one of, if not *the* most ultra-liberal countries in the world in economic terms, while a terror system of rule was installed. That was a weird combination: ultra-freedom for the powerful, and repression for everybody else. I lived in a state of permanent fear. Some of my colleagues were sent directly from their offices to a detention center where they were tortured, and some disappeared. I could have been one of them, since I was connected to the enemy of the regime and was also an unwelcome woman with a man's profession in a man's world.

Every minute of at least twelve years of the seventeen that the military regime lasted, I felt my life was in danger. I wanted to be a wonderful mother and also have a fulfilling life, but I was filled with fear and rejection. My parents stayed close to me, always criticizing, and almost all the rest of the family turned their backs on me. I did not accept the help my parents offered me. I could not allow myself to owe them anything, since our worlds were so distant in spite of the physical closeness.

Hence, being jobless was not a simple game. And feeling worthless did not make it any better. In addition to being a chemical engineer, I became a systems analyst and had the good fortune to be hired by the IT manager of a bank who had also been originally trained as a chemical engineer. He liked the idea of having a colleague working on his team.

Although I hated the job, I thought of myself as privileged and grateful to have a dignified position as an IT project developer in those difficult times. I even had the opportunity to be hired at another bank, and the money I earned allowed me not to ask for help. That was all that mattered.

Actually I was exhausted, and dragged myself to the office every day. Our working conditions were dour and uncomfortable, and I thought that no one cared to listen to my proposals. In fact, I learned that my boss considered me controversial and a danger to him, although we had been well acquainted as classmates at the university. An inner voice told me that I needed a change, but at the same time I felt I had no options. My professional life seemed to me as good as it would ever get.

My personal life was developing in a similar way. I was pushing (with little energy) a four-year unsatisfactory relationship with someone I knew did not have the will and the strength to cope with a family. I said to myself that at my age (late thirties) I would never find anyone suited to be my life partner. Who would want to be with an old woman with two teenagers?

Transformation

Towards the end of 1986, my life turned upside down. I heard a simple inner calling: "You have to go to this seminar to which you were invited. If needed, you yourself will pay for it!"

The seminar was to be given by a Chilean exile living in California who was allowed to come back to Chile in 1985. I received a rather mysterious invitation. I was only told to be confident that I would live a transformational experience. I was more excited than I had been for years. And my boss allowed me to go!

The speaker offered to show us a methodology and a way of looking at life that would bring us well-being and productivity. And I really believed it. I participated in many exercises, and I was hungry to know more when the event was over. I knew then that someday I would help others do what this remarkable coach had done for me. He opened a new world of possibilities. I found myself craving for something big, shaping a purpose, in spite of the dictatorship, for the first time in my adult life.

I will never know for sure whether what happened after that first seminar was just a coincidence or a demonstration of the power of the universe to connect the dots that link facts and people at the right time. A month later we were told that the CEO of our bank had hired an IT consultant who was Chilean and would be arriving after a long stay in France where he had enjoyed a spectacular career in banking IT. There were all sorts of rumors running at my office, not the least of them that we would be individually tested and could be fired. The consultant met with everyone and had very polite conversations with each one of us in the days before Christmas of 1986.

When we first met, I could not help noticing that he looked surprised. He made some awkward movements with his right arm until finally he extended it and shook hands with me, which is not common in our culture. (We kiss each other's cheeks lightly when a woman and a man meet, even in a working environment.) I looked at him and had two simultaneous internal conversations. One was "It seems he likes me." That kind of assessment was completely out of my repertoire. I had always felt that I was not likable and that I needed to prove that I was worthy of anyone's affection. This time I was shocked to discover that I had impressed him just by my presence.

The second conversation was "In spite of his credentials, he is one of 'my people.'" After thirteen years of dictatorship there was still resistance to it, and the country was divided into "them" and "us" ("us" being the enemy).

During our first interview I asked some indirect questions about his life and connections in France. His answers reassured my intuition. He was one of "ours." As children, and then as singles, we had both lived in the same neighborhood, used the same buses, gone to the same university, and had many common friends, yet had never met. He had arrived in France as an exile without a valid passport or any knowledge of French, and with hardly any money. His resilience helped him develop a good career in IT and finance while raising two children together with his first wife.

Soon after our first professional conversations, he invited me out for tea to converse about our lives and our jobs. I learned that he and his new French wife had come to Chile two weeks earlier. She was much younger than he, had never been married, and had made it clear that she would not take care of his two children who had returned to Chile some months before to live with their mother. Life circumstances forced them to live together with his teenaged children, and the situation was becoming unbearable for everyone.

We started seeing each other every day. I not only felt how much he was attracted to me, but I think, most importantly, that for the first time in any relationship I did not feel judged. He showed an unconditional acceptance and we discovered that we were meant to be together. We frequently said the same thing at the same time, we loved our conversations, and we were bonded by a similar personal history. In March of 1988 we started living together, overcoming several difficult family issues. We later married, and I feel he is still attracted to me to this day, though probably in a different way than in 1986, and I also still feel his unconditional acceptance of me. Nobody has ever supported me in the way he has. Never again did I fantasize about being financially miserable.

After all, life did send me the four children I had dreamed of having, and we are now the happy grandparents of seven. With his support and my passion for expanding and improving the worlds of others, I started thinking bigger and bigger and have been able to hold leadership positions that had been out of the question before raising my self-confidence and taking coaching training with my husband's support.

Today I am creating my own dreams for a better world and starting new ways to fulfill them. Regardless of whether he understands all my actions, my husband still accepts me and supports me just the way he did back in 1987 when we were building our relationship. And my coaching masters and trainers gave me the skills and instilled a passion that is just as strong as it was between 1987 and 1991 when I was training.

This story shows me the power of love, acceptance, and passion to transform a life. The universe offers each of us everything we need for fulfillment and transformation. We just need to open up and receive these wonderful gifts.

Sally Bendersky is an experienced transformational coach and strategic consultant. Having been on both sides of the fence as a coach and a leader, she is passionate about creating organizations that encourage human beings to access their full potential while developing quality relationships and professional skills. Sally is the author of the forthcoming book, *The Novel Entrepreneur: A Heart-Centered Path for Fulfillment.* Visit www.SallyBCoach.com and join her in the effort to build humane companies with fulfilled people.

When Being "Not Good Enough" Is Not Good Enough

Karen, Kyloon, and Me

PITIFUL CRIES EMERGE FROM MY SOUL. How can one person exist in a single body with so many conflictions and dichotomies? Superior verbal intelligence and a master's degree, yet my memory and processing speed are that of an eighty-year-old. My body looks young, but aches from previously crushed bones. My soul is torn. My inner child is lost. I push beyond my physical capacity and cry nightly. Is there help for my soul?

Have you ever felt the emotions I just described above? Have you ever thought you were beyond repair and that to commit suicide was the only way to escape from your internal negative voices? Well, Karen, Kyloon, and Me, the authors of this story, want to tell you their story about finding freedom from self-hatred and rediscovering self-acceptance through the love of God.

One might read this and think that I am schizophrenic, but I am not. The mind plays tricks on even the healthiest of minds, and makes accommodations to make life easier for the host – me, Karen, the adult. This is the story of how Karen, the adult, gets to agree with Kyloon, the survivor-self, and finally meets Karen, the inner child, to become one person, a whole being, conquering fears together.

"He healeth the broken in heart, and bindeth up their wounds."
— Psalm 147:3

"How can I be feeling rejected when I don't want to go back to that toxic relationship?" "Who is talking or feeling this way?" These were questions that resonated in my mind, and I wanted to find the answers. One night I woke up to feel the child within my heart crying. Holding my hand to my heart, I spoke to the child within and told her emphatically that I would take care of her. The very next morning I called my counselor and asked if we could meet that same day. That was the day we had the experience of meeting the little girl within. This little girl had been locked up inside me for forty-one years and decided it was now time to emerge from her prison. Did she feel a sense of security or even a newfound sense of independence? (I feel the child felt that her host, Karen, was healed enough to allow the child's voice to be heard.)

Sitting in my counsellor's office, I told her my intention of letting that little girl out. I stood up and said I needed a hug. Tears started to stream down my face. A frightened child emerged, crying as we hugged. Words like "I was so scared; I was so alone" came out of my mouth. I, Karen, also said, "She is so dynamic." The whole process took about two minutes. Teary-eyed, my counselor said, "Thank you for allowing me to be a part of that experience. Who is this little girl and what's her name?" I answered, "This is me as a child, who didn't want to be seen. Everyone saw Kyloon, the strong one who could overcome everything. It is I, the frightened little girl, who was not good enough."

I'd been in counselling for the past year uncovering the many destructive layers of a verbally abusive marriage that kept me captive within my own soul. I would not have tried to reach the frightened, hurt child without my counsellor's help. And the child within had been so scared that she had not wanted to come out unprotected. She wanted to be with someone who understood her, knew her, and loved her.

Now Karen, the frightened child, wanted to be heard. These are some of her feelings that she had kept locked up inside for so long. She wanted to be heard in order to let them go.

I am not good enough. I cannot walk straight as a result of the accident.
I am not good enough. I cannot learn as well as my sisters.
I am not good enough. I have a paralyzed hand that does not work.
I am not good enough. I have seizures.
I am not good enough. I am not pretty.
I am not good enough. I am fat.
I am not good enough. I cannot do anything well enough for my father.
I am not good enough. I cannot be accepted by my father.
I am not good enough. I'm stupid.
I am not good enough. I don't know how to dress.
I am not good enough. I don't know how to do anything right.
I am not good enough. I cannot stand up to my ex's anger.
I am not good enough. I cannot stand up to my daughter's anger.
I am not good enough. I could not stand up to my father's anger.

These are only a few of the lies I told myself. These kinds of voices only separate you from the love of God and His truth, of whom you really are and who you really will become.

"For we are his workmanship, created in Christ Jesus unto good works, which God hath before ordained that we should walk in them."
— Ephesians 2:10

That night as I slept and woke as I do every night, the little girl awakened in me. But the next morning I felt as if there were a giant hole in my chest. I realized that for the first time in so many years I didn't feel the pain that had occupied that portion of my heart. Being a Christian and knowing God's love, I knew there was only one thing I had to do: Fill the hole with new and positive experiences.

*"Be Blessed as God fills up the hole in your heart, those empty places,
that bottomless pit that craves nearness, intimacy, affirmation,
connection, significance, yet fears it is unable to receive it,
and runs away from it."*
− 2008, Sylvia Gunther, The Father's Business

Kyloon, the survivor, who had always led the way, finally realized that she was killing the host, Karen, the adult. She loved her too much to hurt her anymore. She had to step down in order for Karen to take care of herself. Kyloon had brought Karen through hell and back twice now in Karen's life. Once, after the accident, bringing her back to a physical life; and the other when she contemplated suicide during her seventeen-year verbally abusive marriage. Going a million miles an hour, teaching up to twelve hours a day, and pushing herself to achieve her self-worth was no longer working.

Karen, the adult, had to stop running and take care of her broken body by herself. She had to embrace and love herself as she was. If not, I, Kyloon, would kill her by always pushing her beyond what she was physically capable of doing.

I Ran to My Broken Body to Create a Whole Being

After many internal arguments with myself, I finally walked through the doors of a physician's office. I wanted answers. I was referred for a complete neuropsychological exam to evaluate the brain trauma from being struck down by a car going fifty-five miles an hour when I was eleven years old. Forty-seven years later I was finally being tested. The brain injury, which resulted as I flew into the windshield of the car, kept me in a coma for three days.

After the test, an occupational therapy specialist was recommended by my neurologist to do another six-hour examination to further evaluate my brain dysfunction. Afterwards she clearly explained my condition to me and used visual aids to show me where my problems were and how I needed to take care of them. She showed me a picture of a teapot. During the day, the teapot (my brain) runs out of water quickly, at which point I can no longer work on memory problems and can fry my brain. This leads to extreme fatigue, which I often feel at the end of the day. If I don't refuel by allowing myself breaks as often as every fifteen minutes, I can hurt my brain. I was killing myself. This I knew.

I had set up a lifestyle that was taking care of many of the deficits in my brain. This is why I am so good at teaching kids with disabilities. I have that "been there, done that" kind of mentality. I know all the tricks of the trade to help these kids succeed. I was fine until I reached my older years; then my foundation began to shake.

Now, finally, Karen, the adult, is ready to take on her responsibility. Kyloon must step to one side, cheering on Karen, the adult, while Karen, the child, stands beside her on the other side. Karen is ready to step up on the podium and introduce herself as a whole being.

I can finally express these words: "I am a whole being." Karen, the child; Kyloon, the survivor; and Karen, the adult, have reunited. I am free of pain in my chest. I have noticed a childish personality emerging who loves to dream. I remember her imagination and energy. My journey is to love all of me, take care of what I have, and honor and respect every part of me, broken or not. By loving and honoring my body, soul, and mind, I can honor God, my Lord and Savior, all the greater. I can do this from a healed heart, which I have been searching for all my adult life.

With God's patience, love, and direction, I am now able to continually seek refuge and healing in God's arms while listening to His sweet voice.

I am so thankful that I decided to search for, find, love, and ultimately let go of my own internal monsters while seeking a deeper relationship with God. I am thankful that I have learned how to love, honor, and accept myself fully as God sees me rather than run away from the pain. Thank you, Lord, for your unconditional Love.

"Though one may be overpowered by another, two can defend themselves. And a threefold cord is not quickly broken."
— Ecclesiastes 4:12

Epilogue

At the age of fifty-eight, I have gained great insight, knowledge, and wisdom from my journey through living with disabilities, verbal abuse, divorce, forgiveness, and self-love. The most difficult challenge for me was to forgive myself for the many mistakes I made and the weaknesses I possess. My survivor-counterpart, Kyloon, constantly reminds me that I must love myself unconditionally, at all times. The child within reminds me to love life at its fullest.

As I finished writing this chapter, I realized that I had not fully walked in the truth of that which I had written. My present teaching assignment has provoked me to step down from teaching after thirty years. My superiors see my weaknesses as failures, and their persecutions and complaints cause me internal pain and discomfort. Once again I feel "NOT GOOD ENOUGH."

My plan is to step down from this teaching job to take a lesser role of helper in the classroom. With my new role and position, I know I can succeed and not feel as if I am a failure. As I wait for this to happen, fear and grief grip my soul, yet I have peace beyond understanding.

If I had decided to fight with my internal ego, Kyloon, and not step down to honor me, Karen, the adult, then yes, I would be a failure. I know God has a greater purpose for me to serve others with His love according to His plan, not mine. I, me, the child, realized this truth the moment I opened my eyes from the coma at age eleven. God had a plan for my life.

God's plan and purpose for your life and mine includes health, prosperity, and love. Are you willing to accept it? God's love never fails when we walk according to His purpose!

40

Karen, a mom, grandmother, author, and teacher, who successfully graduated with a degree in psychology and a master's in education, spends much of her time helping women caught in dark worlds of unending negative voices. Using her life's testimony and book, *Clean Heart,* Karen teaches classes to women who are seeking freedom and healing from their troubled souls through God's love and word. If interested to know more, contact Karen at her website, www. CleanHeartBook.com.

Saved by Accident

Toti Cadavid

IT WAS ABOUT 2:15AM, THANKSGIVING DAY, 2009, when my husband, Luis, and I left the home of a close childhood friend and his wife. We were visiting his native Puerto Rico with our children to spend the holiday with my in-laws. We were in great spirits when we got into the van after a fantastic night of laughter looking at old pictures and reminiscing about our teenage years and the many fun occasions we had shared with other friends back in our native Colombia. It was raining very heavily and we had a fifty-minute drive to the beach house where we were staying. As Luis drove, I tried to stay awake, but the fatigue of the long day got the best of me and I quickly fell asleep.

Suddenly a violent impact jolted me awake, my head and shoulders propelling sideways and then forward towards the dashboard like a crash test dummy. Completely disoriented, I tried to get a sense of what had happened, but it was totally dark inside the van and all around us, and the few highway lights in that area were far away from the place we had crashed.

"What happened?" I asked Luis in a panic.

"We crashed," he replied. "Are you okay?"

"I think so. Are you okay?" I asked.

43

He didn't answer right away, which nearly stopped my heart in my chest. "Yes," he finally said, in a very weak and broken voice.

Luis had lost control of the vehicle in the heavy rain. The van had slid into a mountainside going sixty miles per hour, but by some type of divine intervention, we did not hit it head on. The right front tire collided with a large, protruding rock that jutted out from the mountain and had anchored the vehicle from running full force into it. That rock saved our lives. If we had crashed at any other angle, we would have hit the face of the mountain at full speed, colliding with it on the passenger side where I was seated, and I would most likely not be sharing this story.

I tried to open my door, but something was preventing it from moving. Eventually I made my way out through the side door behind my seat. My foot quickly sank into the mud to just above my ankle. I didn't even know it was broken until I tried to pull it out of the mud and felt the excruciating pain. "Something is wrong with my foot," I yelled to Luis. I painfully pulled my foot out of the mud and limped my way from the wreckage trying to get to where Luis, still disoriented, was standing behind the van. We stood in silence looking at the scene and at what was left of the vehicle. It was only for a few minutes, but it felt like an eternity because of the numerous thoughts racing through our minds. The pain in my foot kept increasing, so Luis helped me into the back seat.

We had been very lucky. After such a major accident, I walked away alive with just a fissured vertebra in my neck and a fractured foot. Luis survived it with several bruises and some cuts to his arms and face, but no serious injuries. The crash, the scene at the hospital, the moment we finally saw our children again, and the rest of Thanksgiving felt surreal. I cried a lot that day... and during the days and months that followed. That unexpected encounter with death made me understand how vulnerable we all are and how easily life can be gone when you least expect it. That day I realized who and what really mattered in my life.

44

A Part of Me Died and Another Was Born

I tried to continue with life as usual when we got home to Denver, but I couldn't. There was something inside of me preventing me from mentally going back to my old life and following my old dreams, which now seemed irrelevant. My job, which had once been a joy to me, had now become a chore. Inside I was dying to get away from the marketing agency I was running, but how could I do that? I had far too many responsibilities and work commitments: contracts to fulfill, brands to launch, and a team to lead. On top of that, we were a two-income family. So I forced myself out of the house every day, attended every meeting, fulfilled every client request, and led my team the best I could. But I kept dying inside, a little bit each day.

Eventually I fell into a deep depression. Things got so bad that I started losing everything from clients to employees, and almost my marriage. So I did what I have always done when life brings me trials and tribulations; I immersed myself in self-help books which had always enlightened me and helped me get through rough periods. However, this time the books were raising even more questions for me. It was as if all those leading authors had conspired to provide me with more questions than answers. I obviously needed additional help, so I started seeing a psychologist, a life coach, a business coach, and a career coach, and began understanding myself more deeply through my first course in neuro-linguistic programming (NLP).

The problem was that the more I learned and the more clarity I acquired, the more I questioned my actions, my decisions, and myself. The more I asked myself *why* I had taken certain actions and made decisions that shaped the direction of my life, the further my heart moved from my marketing career. As I continued to become disconnected from my career and business, the more I kept losing. I found myself swindled by questionable business deals, partnerships, and transactions. I needed help.

45

Eventually I developed a new business partnership, relaunched the agency with a larger scope of work, and put a great deal of pressure on myself to produce higher results. Our team managed to land some large client accounts, but the sad truth was that my heart just wasn't in it anymore – and the clients were feeling it.

During the hours, days, and months after the accident, my brush with death made me realize that everything I had worked so hard for and cared so much about up to that point wouldn't even matter upon my passing. The only thing that would be important was the difference I had or hadn't made in the lives of those I loved. I pictured my children's lives without me and realized that they would grow up with very limited memories of their mother. I could imagine my best friends telling them, "Your mom tried to be a good mother, a savvy business person, a loyal friend, sister, and daughter, but she always felt that she didn't have enough time because she had so many other things on her plate. So she gave all of us a little, but gave her work a lot."

I had failed everyone who was important in my life, because for too long I had either negatively affected or not affected (which is even sadder) all of them: my kids, husband, family, friends, employees, and community. Worst of all I had badly neglected myself and given too much to my career.

Most of what had seemed so important before the accident now seemed trivial. Before I knew it, I simply couldn't keep going as I had before. I was totally drained. I left my own company in the summer of 2012, telling my husband and business partner that I couldn't do it any longer. I did not know what path I was going to take; I just knew that I needed to find myself and do something meaningful with my life.

What Matters? Who Matters?

I had never considered myself a very religious person. In fact, I became very resentful towards God during some very hard years of my life. As a result of my quest and what I learned, I became deeply spiritual. I now believe that we are all put on earth for a reason, to learn specific lessons and find a way to serve others with our unique talents. I have come to understand that all of my challenges and struggles have happened *for* me, not *to* me.

Being so close to death gave me a new perspective on life. I wished I could change everything and do it all differently. I wanted to ask forgiveness from all of the loved ones I had taken for granted for so many years. But would they even welcome me back into their lives? Would they give me another chance? How could I mend the years of wrongdoing and, even worse, of non-doing? These questions made me become completely committed to mending the relationships with everyone in my life, myself included. I needed to live a life that really mattered, making a true impact on the lives of as many people as I could reach.

What Had Driven My Life So Far?

Why did God give me this second chance? What type of life was I living before the accident, and why had it made me so unhappy? I kept going back over the previous twenty-one years to analyze my choices and the reasons behind them throughout the different stages of my life. I kept imagining how things would have been different had I made other decisions. I kept asking myself what had driven me to make the choices I had made. Why didn't I pursue my dream of becoming a journalist? Why did I leave my country, marry my first husband, and have my first child at such a young age? Instead of being grateful, why was I so resentful of God for giving me a special needs son with so many health issues? Why did I leave corporate America? What made me want to become an entrepreneur? What prompted me to get married again? What about my career kept me in it for so long only to become disenchanted after so much hard work? So many questions...

Sadly, all the answers were pointing to the unfortunate truth that I had been living someone else's dreams and ideas of success. I had kept striving to achieve more, thinking that more possessions, awards, and recognition would finally bring me happiness. However, the happiness those things brought didn't last very long. I kept creating higher and harder goals for myself and worked hard to achieve them. I attained what I now refer to as "empty success" – the type that is just material and will never really make anyone happy. It was success generated from goals that were chosen from the outside in instead of the inside out – empty goals that only caused more voids in my life. Although these were very sad realizations, they did give me the immense desire to finally live life on my own terms.

My Next Chapter

That near-death experience threw me into the worst time of my life, but also gave me the opportunity to reclaim myself. I changed a great deal, and with that everything around me changed too. I can now say that I am a truly authentic and much more present, compassionate, patient, and caring individual. I am extremely grateful to have a new opportunity at life. Now my relationships with God, life, family, friends, and everything around me are amazingly different. I finally have the right priorities in place and my heart vibrates with love in different ways every day.

As I found *me,* I found my true purpose. I now dedicate my life to helping people who have somehow lost their way, as I once did. I assist them in discovering what they really want out of life, how to get out of their own way to be able to make it happen, and how to start living a life that feels extraordinary, authentic, free, peaceful, and filled with joy and happiness.

A near-death experience prompted **Toti** to end her successful nineteen-year career as a high-level marketing executive and entrepreneur that saw her manage well-known brands around the world. Through her company, U-Fulfilled, she is now living her passion of empowering individuals to take control of their lives and careers, discover their true purpose, and overcome limitations that have kept them from achieving their dreams. Visit www.U-Fulfilled.com for the free report, *7 Steps to Discovering Your Authentic Self.*

⌒♃⌒

Cultivating Gratitude:
The Seven Signs from Heaven

J. K. Chua, BA (Eng.), MBA

I BELIEVE IN MIRACLES, SERENDIPITY, human fortitude, and perseverance. I strongly believe that if we cultivate a grateful attitude in life, we are more likely to be spiritually strong and enjoy good health and happiness. When we are grateful, we naturally become more reasonable and have more modest expectations of life. We become easily contented and it sets the foundation for happiness.

The First Sign from Heaven appeared in 1976 when my paternal grandmother died. I was turning thirteen that year and Mamma (my name for my grandmother) had suffered from poor health for six months. I still remember Mum and Dad searching for, and exhausting, the local store's limited supply of Sustagen® nutritional supplement beverage to feed Mamma. She depended on that liquid beverage for sustenance in her last days.

When she passed away, we were very sad and I was deeply affected by her death. It was even harder going through the solemn and traditional wake that made it even more depressing. Many of us teared up when we went through the rituals that were steeped in tradition and very much focused on Confucian filial piety.

What made Mamma's death so much easier for us to bear was the fact that she passed away so peacefully. During my grandparents' generation and the generation before, most of the clansmen were illiterate, but they were deeply religious and followed traditional ways. They spoke the Chaozhou (Teochew) dialect and were originally from the Chenghai district of the city of Shantou, Guangdong Province, People's Republic of China. They migrated to Malaya (what is now Malaysia) in the 1920s. They retained many of the traditional values and beliefs passed down from their ancestors in China. They believed that "The good, the kind, and the religious die peacefully with no suffering at all."

As the burning white candles melted during the wake at our ancestral home, the wax miraculously formed the shape of the Goddess of Mercy. This fortuitous occurrence would suggest that Mamma was in heaven. Even the burning joss sticks soon formed curves flowing down like willow branches that the Goddess of Mercy was often depicted holding.

My grandfather was extremely pleased with Mamma's pleasant appearance in death. Choked with emotion, he looked at her and said, "Well, you have left us so peacefully. Don't forget to 'look after' your children and grandchildren."

She was a most devoted wife and mother, and an equally loving and kind grandmother. Being the religious person she was, she never failed to pray for her family's safety, good health, and well-being.

The Second Sign from Heaven appeared in 1997 when I was summoned home from a business trip in North America. I had to return home immediately to be with my Mum, who was comatose due to brain meningitis. Her condition was grave and even the doctors who attended to her did not dare speculate on the prognosis or her ability to recover.

I was in Ottawa, Canada, with my wife, and transiting to Orlando, Florida, to attend the Nortel Users Conference when my sister left me the voicemail about my Mum on my office phone. I did not have a mobile phone at the time. A few days earlier I had missed a weekly call to my parents and I felt guilty about it, as I might have prevented the situation had I spoken with Mum – I could have encouraged her to see a doctor earlier. Although Mum had not been feeling well, she took her condition too lightly and refused to see the doctor until it was too late.

Nevertheless, we prayed for Mum to recover from her condition. Our close family members also rallied around us with emotional support and daily prayers. After a few weeks she started to show signs of recovery. She finally recovered, and it reaffirmed our belief in divine help. Our prayers had been answered!

For the next few years my wife and I could only vaguely remember the details about my mother's coma. It was as if we were numbed and our brains selectively did not remember the emotionally draining experience. One thing we did remember was the power of prayers.

After my experience with Mum's near-fatal illness, I started to research Buddhism and the subject of life and death. I chanced upon *The Tibetan Book of the Living and Dying* by Sogyal Rinpoche, which helped me overcome my fear of death.

The Third Sign from Heaven appeared in 1999 when we were blessed with our first son and we felt that he was a gift from heaven. He was the proverbial bundle of joy, and brought us immense happiness. I had often prayed for a child after being married for quite a few years, and we were finally blessed with a son. It was indeed a sign from heaven, and my wife and I were grateful to have a child.

The Fourth Sign from Heaven appeared in 2005 when I was diagnosed with non-viral liver hepatitis. I had been afflicted by irritable bowel syndrome for a few months before finding out one day that I was severely jaundiced with hepatitis. I had sludge in my gallbladder and a fatty liver condition that aggravated the situation. I thought that perhaps it was a sign from heaven for me to slow down and take care of my health. I had been very complacent with my physical well-being. I was overworked and ate irregular meals.

I researched on the Internet to see how I could heal myself and started to juice regularly and reduce my intake of oils and sugar. I ate lots of fresh fruits and vegetables, and as a salad dressing I used only extra virgin olive oil and balsamic vinegar. I also began to drink apple cider vinegar regularly.

I started to recover, and even more amazing, the sludge in my gallbladder and the fatty deposits around my liver disappeared. Liver function test markers indicated that my liver was back to its normal self. Even the specialist was surprised by my recovery. He asked what I had done to recover from my condition, and I told him that it was just dieting, juicing, and watching what I ate.

My life had come to a standstill when my hepatitis became life-threatening, but thankfully for the next few years I remained healthy. **The Fifth Sign from Heaven appeared in 2006** when we had our second child, who was yet another bundle of joy just like our firstborn. In fact, he is cherubic even to this day. He brings us joy in the way he endears himself to us and he often comes up with an unexpected question or comment about life. Once he told us that he wanted to rear a puppy. When we asked him why, he told us it was because it was cute and its fur was smooth. He added that he wanted to be responsible and care for a little puppy.

Just the other day my younger son said something interesting while we were out for a drive and he looked out of the car window into the sky. He said that the clouds were so nice that they looked like candy floss. He said that the clouds looked so good that he wanted to eat them, but before that he would need to sprinkle some sugar on them.

Both my wife and I love children and we had silently wished to have another child. Our second one brought immense happiness not only to us but also to my older son. In fact, every time we talked about our second son there was a twinkle in our older boy's eyes. Our older son has a soft spot for his younger brother, especially when his brother is unwell.

The Sixth Sign from Heaven appeared in 2009 when I was diagnosed with kidney cancer. I was in shock but never in denial. I did not ask why this had happened to me, but instead thought through the options.

When I reflected on my condition, I realized that I was still living recklessly when it came to my health. I had not maintained a healthy lifestyle beyond the first two years after I had been diagnosed with hepatitis. I was under exceptional stress at work, which was aggravated when I kept irregular hours and irregular meals. Stress and insufficient sleep became a lethal combination that affected my health.

This was a second wakeup call to take my health seriously and not allow it to deteriorate. I had become complacent and was now being given a third chance to take care of my physical self. I became even more serious about living a healthy life than before.

The Seventh Sign from Heaven appeared in 2013 when my mother passed away. Mum had been on life support for over two months. We prayed hard for her to be weaned off life support and for her recovery, but I dared not expect too much.

Although this time we were better prepared for Mum's grave situation, it was different from 1997 when she had been in a coma. This time the odds were against Mum due to her advanced age and her Parkinson's disease. She finally showed signs of recovery and was comfortable enough to be sent home. Unfortunately she passed away three days later.

I reflected on the lessons I had learned from the experience. First, I learned to be better prepared for the death of a loved one. Second, I learned the importance of making the necessary preparations for death. Third, I realized the importance of spending time with family so that there is no regret after they pass away.

As my uncle had said, Mum's death taught us the lesson to be prepared for our own death. Mum's death taught us to think through the death process. Death, I believe, should be embraced as something that comes naturally in the cycle of life.

For many years I have read and re-read *The Tibetan Book of the Living and Dying*, but its lessons are nothing compared to experiencing firsthand the death of a loved one in appreciating how to accept death as part of life. When I reflected back on the previous year when I had decided to start my own business, I realized that it may have been a sign from heaven to spend time with family.

I am sharing my personal Seven Signs from Heaven that affected me to remind people to pay heed to signs from heaven that can and will affect your life. We often ignore the signs from heaven until it becomes too late to change or make a difference. Often the same signs come repeatedly to us, but we choose to ignore them at our own peril.

J. K. Chua worked in corporate America for twenty-six years. As a mentor, coach, and motivational speaker, he demonstrates passion, commitment, and perseverance to change people's lives. After surviving life-threatening kidney cancer and liver hepatitis, his mission in life is to help people with programs to revitalize their body, reactivate their mind, and rejuvenate their soul so that they can live a great life! Visit www.StartMe.CareerFastStart.com for his free ebook. Visit www.JKCHUA.com, www.HowToLiveAGreatLife.com, and www.CancerPreventionEveryDay.com to be inspired.

Food Affects Everything

Nancy Cooper

THE SECOND DOCTOR'S EXPERT OPINION: "HAVE A HYSTERECTOMY." The surgery would solve all my female problems. I know that many, many worse things have happened to fifty-year-old women, but I was in shock.

I am not fond of doctor's offices. As a child I fainted and dropped clear to the floor while standing in a crowded emergency room after having been given a simple tetanus shot. (Heaven only knows why I was standing, but there you have it.) My reaction was not to the injection itself, but to the thought of the needle. And (this little interlude of a story gets better) I broke my arm as a result of the fall! It must have been an interesting phone conversation when my mom told my dad why we would be extra late for dinner that evening!

Not being a lover of medical procedures from the get-go, I was horrified at the idea of a hysterectomy. So I put on my research hat and got busy on the internet. Thank goodness for that amazing tool. I found out more about lady parts than I had ever known before, and I have two grown children! I also found out about body chemistry, hormones, and what affects them. Food affects the whole body, and we eat multiple times each day.

I still own the six books that were most helpful to me. I found out that I am unique. Instead of diving into all the details of the many possible medical procedures and surgeries, and even the holistic medicine alternatives, I went straight to reading about diet.

As I was reading all these books and doing internet research, a thing called The Engine 2 Immersion, a nutrition education program, came across my radar (computer) screen. My poor, long-suffering husband said, "Go!" So I did.

That weekend in September of 2011 was no less than life-changing. I learned things I had no idea I was there to learn. My diet and my outlook on how what we eat affects our lives went through a change just as transformative as that of a butterfly in metamorphosis. I went home and read all the labels in my pantry. Every box, every bag, every can was scrutinized with the ideas I had learned at the Immersion. Then I hit the refrigerator! Since then nothing in my kitchen has been the same.

During the retreat, Rip Esselstyn, founder of the program, said, "The bad foods you love aren't loving you back. You're in an abusive relationship." Well, I do not tolerate abuse in other areas of my life, so why should I tolerate it in what I eat every day, several times a day?

I put two and two together. I looked honestly at my state of health and what my Standard American Diet (SAD) consisted of. I added those observations to what I had learned during the three-day Immersion, and believed what Rip had said. I enjoy cooking and had always liked my pantry, but its contents had betrayed me. Now I was going to have to take charge and insert some love and respect into our relationship!

A Totally New Way to Feel

As I adapted to a whole foods, plant-based way of eating, I was amazed that almost immediately I felt better and had more energy.

When the doctor had asked how I was feeling, I remember telling her I felt draggy, lethargic, and a bit dizzy at times, perhaps for the past seven years. Apparently I had become accustomed to this state of being. It finally became unbearable and I sought medical help. Not cool. I have learned that falling apart as we age in this culture is normal, but it is absolutely not natural and not necessary.

My female problems improved, and it took a bit of time but I went into menopause without having to go through any kind of drug regimen, procedure, or surgery.

If I had to live through many years of ill health in order to find and embrace the whole foods, plant-based way of eating, then so be it. I am grateful. My health is better now than it was twenty years ago. I have the stamina to do all the things I want to do and keep up with any crazy dream I can come up with!

I am not saying that every woman, given similar circumstances, is able to totally avoid drugs, procedures, or surgery. However, what I know for sure (as Oprah would say) is that adopting a whole foods, plant-based way of eating can help lessen, prevent, and even cure many chronic medical problems that have become common and even normal in our culture.

And Thus the Story Begins

I have become angry – at times red-faced, stompin', stuttering angry – about all the years I spent lost in the ignorance of feeding my own beautiful children the Standard American Diet. I now know why I was largely unsuccessful at providing my children with the healthiest diet possible. I was clueless until the Engine 2 Immersion. And what I have since learned, not just about health but about life in general, is that the answers are always somewhere.

We cannot go back to life as usual once we have found even one good clue as to how to have the life we want. We can try to ignore that small clue, but once we find it, it is forever in the background of our lives, waiting to come out and be put to good use. We cannot erase it from the databanks in our minds and hearts.

Nothing we do in life is neutral, so we have two choices: Sink into life-denying victimhood, or get busy and go deep into life-affirming, radical, obnoxious digging for whatever information we need. We dig deep to find the answers that will lead to the clarity and joy we wish for ourselves.

What I Found Out

I dug in. I signed up for programs; attended classes and conferences, both online and in person; read and absorbed and gained knowledge. I cannot pretend that I do not know what I know. I believe my own children would have been healthier had I known thirty years ago what I know now. I know their lives would be simpler and healthier today had they developed the habit of whole foods, plant-based eating as they were growing up.

Each and every time we give our precious children a non-nutritional food-like product to eat, we are depriving them of the life-giving, muscle and brain-developing nutrients they need to grow into the brightest, most successful, happiest human beings they were born to be.

We are not being taught to properly feed ourselves and our loved ones. We do not learn sustainable, healthy nutrition in our schools, at home, in doctor's offices, or from the numerous organizations and governmental entities we have grown to trust. There is something desperately missing from our dietary system – communication and a general willingness on the part of the public to face the problem and dig in.

Disease prevention is the most important subject with which to start the food conversation. How do we lessen the effects of the infections, autoimmune diseases, allergies, weight problems, and learning difficulties that are brought about by the malnutrition that is rampant in our society? Western medicine is best when it comes to treating critical and acute problems, but it falls sorely short when treating our many chronic maladies and illnesses. Symptoms of disease are treated, but very often causes of disease are not.

For several years I have felt as if I know a great secret. Remember the movie *The Secret*? Well never mind that; I know the *real* secret! And I feel it should be shouted from the rooftops! The real secret is that what we eat affects everything. It affects how we feel and the amount of energy we have, and thereby the very enthusiasm we have for life itself. What we eat affects how we treat one another, from our loved ones to the people in our world whom we are not so fond of. We must ask ourselves if we have the health and stamina to deal positively and effectively with the circumstances and events in our daily lives. Are we able to be the people we wish to be in the world, or are we hampered by our health conditions?

What we eat also affects the animals on our planet and our very beautiful planet itself. But those are stories for another chapter!

Grandma Bear

We are all familiar with the idea of the fierce and protective mama bear. When my granddaughter was born, my daughter-in-law turned into the best mama bear I know! As I watch my son's wonderful family grow in love and light, I enjoy my new role as Grandma Bear. I don't think it quite works this way with bears in the wild, but I am ready to take on anything that comes close to threatening the health and happiness of my granddaughter. I believe the biggest immediate threats to her health and happiness today are the misguided ideas and practices regarding the food and food-like substances we consume on a daily basis.

I have learned and experienced that adopting a whole foods, plant-based way of eating is the healthiest, most sustainable way for humans to live. As a result of eating this way, I am secure in knowing that as I grow older, I will not suffer from obesity, diabetes, heart disease, high blood pressure, crippling arthritis, dementia, or any other common chronic disease. I know that my chances of having to deal with cancer are vastly reduced because of my food choices. But more important than any of those things, I have learned that if we modify what our children eat every day, we can prevent them from having to suffer through most of the side effects of strong drugs and medical procedures used to treat many of today's common maladies and diseases. Too many children miss school and other activities due to time spent sitting in doctor's offices and hospitals with preventable chronic diseases.

Inertia is a killer when it comes to our health and that of our loved ones. Don't stay stuck. Don't accept chronic illness as an inevitable part of life. The heck with remaining an ignorant victim! Dig in to find out where our health problems come from. And when you find a clue, follow it like a bloodhound… or like a grandma bear!

Nancy Cooper believes all parents should adopt the healthiest diet for their children. She has started this vital conversation by becoming a clearinghouse for clarity on the subject of whole foods, plant-based eating. She is the author of the upcoming book, *Children's Healthiest Diet: On Purpose Plant-Based Eating.* Nancy invites parents, caregivers, and anyone else responsible for feeding our children (and therefore directly responsible for their health as well) to join her at www.ChildrensHealthiestDiet.com.

The Gold in the Darkness

Pam Culley-McCullough, EdD

MY DAD SLEPT QUIETLY IN THE HOSPITAL bed situated in his living room. He didn't have long to live. With hospice caregivers gone for the day, I was with him for the evening. As he slept and I settled in, I began to reflect on our relationship of forty-seven years as father and daughter along with our many trials and joys. My family definitely had had its share of obstacles, most notably my dad's many years of alcoholism, but luckily we experienced the joy of his recovery, too. Each challenge had seemed not only unexpected, but very unwanted at the time. Yet now I was beginning to see that the lessons learned couldn't have prepared me better to be there now with my dad as I faced our last big challenge together: his death and our final separation.

The challenge to be open to the dying process was very new to me. Nine years before, my mom had died suddenly from an apparent aneurism on the back side of her heart. One day she was there and the next day she wasn't. The suddenness left no time to say good-bye. The shock left me paralyzed, without words or understanding, let alone the possibility of closure, for quite some time. Now, even though my dad had lived with cancer for four years, and yes, we'd had time to talk about a lot of things, I still had to prepare for the inevitable loss. Once again, the magnitude of this loss had sent me into a tailspin. I was beside myself with sorrow.

63

I tried to steady myself as I took a few deep breaths. Even though my heart continued its familiar ache, my feelings began to settle. I then decided to read one of the books I had brought with me for the evening. I turned to a series of meditations and was drawn to one focused on the idea of letting go. Yes, I certainly needed help there. As I began to read, I felt the power of the message.

Taking a break, I looked over at my dad for a moment. He was now awake. Just as I was about to ask him if he needed anything, he said to me in a very lucid voice, "Honey, I like that passage, too – the one about letting go." How had he known what I was reading? I hadn't said a word. Still perplexed, I read the passage he said he liked as a way to double-check. "Yes," he said, "That was the one." Realistically, we both knew this couldn't be happening... but it was. Suddenly our eyes locked, and I felt a strange, otherworldly energy that seemed to be from Spirit confirming that indeed we were communicating in a new way, telepathically, and that our relationship would continue even after death. Without saying another word, we clearly knew something BIG and unexpected had just happened.

The big and unexpected had been a constant theme in my family when I was growing up. On the outside we appeared to be a normal suburban family, but on the inside the inherited legacy of alcoholism from my dad's alcoholic parents set the stage. For my dad, the embarrassment and shame from his childhood were ever-present, the humiliation deeply internalized. He vowed to never be affected by this curse, and in so doing he stuffed his pain away and focused instead on promoting his career and providing for his family. Yes, he had good intentions, but without realizing it he had already been seduced by the effects of alcohol. In his youth alcohol had been central to his enjoyment, whether he was at a private party or a company-sanctioned event. Yet afterward he always felt remorse – once again he had failed to control himself. He thought he just needed a stronger resolve. But with alcohol he could silence the taunting demons within and be the life of the party. He didn't have to hear the demons' frequent taunts saying, "You'll never be good enough or smart enough." By day he worked hard trying to outrun the emotional pain, and even achieved great success in his career, but by night alcohol captured him. Instead of being an elixir, alcohol quickly became his jailer... and ours as well.

Having my family organized around addiction created a crazy world of its own. This is easy for me to see now, but when I was younger I didn't even know it was an addiction, let alone what the long-term impact would later be on our lives. It was normal for my dad to come home from work smelling of stale cigarette smoke and with alcohol on his breath, his gait unsteady, speech slurred, and eyes glazed over, and for my mom and I to wonder if he had sideswiped a neighbor's car on the way home. It was normal for my mom to be agitated with anger, seething beneath her seemingly calm veneer when she saw his "demeanor" as she called it (aka drunkenness). It was normal for one of my parents to erupt at the dinner table, either my dad spouting off about some injustice he felt (and making no sense whatsoever) or my mom finding an opening to deliver a scathing criticism of my dad's behavior (always short, but never sweet). Out of desperation I would add to the frenzy by lashing out at my dad, taking advantage of his altered state. Afterward I would feel disgusted, not only with him, but with myself. Never did the crisis end in physical abuse. Instead we each went quietly to our respective rooms for the rest of the evening like nothing had happened. My dad was basically a functioning alcoholic. He was able to run his own million-dollar business for years without major incident, yet this was the water we swam in for many years, not knowing we were drowning.

Addiction can happen to such good people, and my dad was one of them. He was funny, smart, and capable of such love. I adored him, but most of the time my feelings zigzagged from embarrassment and disappointment to anger and contempt. Eventually all I could feel was despair.

I attended my first Al-Anon meeting in my late twenties. By then I had hit my emotional bottom, once I had returned home from graduate school and witnessed the devastating effects of this disease on my parents. It was worse than I had ever imagined. However, I finally accepted that I couldn't save my family even though part of me desperately wanted to. First and foremost, I needed to save myself.

From that point on I became committed to my own healing. With the help of Al-Anon, competent and caring therapists, and the reading of many excellent books targeting alcoholism, I began my long journey. Going slowly into the darkness of my own pain, I began to understand the many sorrows housed within me. Receiving great care and support during this time, I looked deeply at every sorrow, one by one. By shining light on each hurt, I was able to see for the first time the "gold" that remained once healing had occurred. The first nugget of gold gave me the courage to find my voice, and once I found my voice, my chronic, low-grade depression, common in many alcoholic families, lifted. Deep feelings of hopelessness, low energy, and little self-confidence abated. I was free to fully be in my life without compromise. Slowly my emotional life became balanced, and I began to feel moments of joy and happiness for the first time.

Yet my dad continued to drink. And my mom became more and more desperate. No matter how deep my despair, I continued to try to find an opportunity for greater growth for myself. One day an opportunity came to have a formal conversation with both of my parents about my dad's addiction and its effect on our family. It was time to finally speak the truth about what was happening to us. I wanted something better for my family. Aside from that, I had no further control. It took many attempts, but finally my dad entered a month-long rehabilitation program on his own volition at the age of sixty-five.

My mom and I entered into my dad's recovery process with cautious optimism. My dad embraced it! He immersed himself in learning all he could about the disease and his vulnerability to it. He confronted his demons and made peace within and with others. He lived by AA's 12-step program, eventually becoming one of the leaders of the group. He never looked back. He said he felt free of his inner demons for the first time ever.

It was then that I asked him for much-needed time for us to begin to mend our torn and tattered relationship. We spent time talking, writing, and sharing. He made himself available as best he could. In time our hearts began to mend, and as a result I discovered more gold nuggets in the form of compassion and forgiveness. I had my dad back for the first time in many years. It wasn't perfect, but it was a beginning.

Then the sudden death of my mother two years later signaled an unprecedented transition like none I had known. All of my beliefs were thrown into question. I immersed myself in a search for answers about life and death... and so did my dad. We shared our discoveries over time and found solace in our many philosophical conversations.

But when my dad was diagnosed with cancer, I became frozen in fear. My dad was speechless. Nevertheless he completed all of the recommended treatment options. But when those options were exhausted and the cancer remained, I discovered the true meaning of surrender... not giving in, but opening up to whatever lessons were necessary at that time. My dad appreciated that insight as well. Through our tears we said all we needed to say. Our hearts opened further. My dad even talked about what death might be about. But no matter what was imagined, we both believed his passing would be our final good-bye. With this understanding I tried to face our last days together with grace.

Just when I thought there wasn't anything more to open to, Spirit stepped in suggesting that death would not be our final separation. Could this be true?

Once my dad died, I was immersed in my grief. My heart was closed to anything other than my tears. Then one day I remembered what Spirit had promised. Wanting to find out if there was any truth to the promise, I asked my dad to give me a sign if our relationship was meant to continue. I held this question in my mind as I went on my usual morning walk. Not really expecting a response, I wasn't surprised when my walk came to an end and nothing had happened. No voice, no sign. Just as I let go of the idea altogether, I looked down at the ground. There at the base of my driveway was a large, magnificent feather like none I had ever seen before. Now, feathers are dear to my heart, and I treasure any I find. I see them as messages from Spirit. But I knew this feather had not been there when I began my walk. Once I picked it up and held it to my heart, I knew my question had been answered. Death would not be our final separation.

Since then I have had ongoing communication with my dad. Healing has continued as I "talk" with him often. Without the experiences of the past could either of us have been ready for this call from Spirit as he lay dying? If our hearts had not healed and become open to our love for one another, could this unexpected vein of gold ever have been received? Maybe not. But what I know for sure is that love and forgiveness transformed us, each in our own way and in our own time, and gave us the precious and unexpected gift of continued connection.

After retiring from a successful thirty-year career as a psychologist, **Pam Culley-McCullough, EdD,** heeded her inner spirit calling her to write the soon-to-be-published book, *The Gold in the Darkness*. In this riveting book she chronicles her father's journey through alcoholism to recovery, and the unexpected transformation that led to their eventual afterlife connection. To join her community and follow her blog, go to www.ConversationsWithPoppy.com.

It's a Matter of Trust

Susan L. Dascenzi, MSW, LCSW

December 27, 1992

"HEY GIRLFRIEND, I CAN SHOW YOU WHAT GOD'S *really* all about." Those words would haunt me for years. I had no idea what he meant by that statement which he uttered in a drunken stupor, but my gut knew... and I didn't listen.

"Okay guys. It's three a.m. Closing time. You have to go now," I said as I removed the last few glasses of watered-down liquor from the bar. I had my handy barkeep's rag and began clearing the evidence of their rambunctious partying. *Why didn't I know?* My two regulars, who always stayed with me until they were the last ones to leave, stood up, grabbed their six-pack from the cooler, and stopped in the middle of the long U-shaped bar to pay. *He* was still sitting on the far side of the bar – away from the door. "Come on, let's go – you have to leave now, too."

Even though he'd consumed a few too many and he was a "friend" of the other two regulars from their old high school days, I figured he would leave when they did. *What is wrong with this gut of mine? What is it trying to tell me?*

As my two regulars started walking toward the door, so did he. *Good, he's leaving with them.* As my regulars left the bar, *He* stopped and said to me, "Aw, come on, one more?" As I said, "No, you've got to go.

69

It's three-fifteen in the morning," and glanced down at my watch, I felt the first crushing blow. I literally didn't know what hit me. *What's happening? Why is my head hurting?*

As the blows continued, I reached for anything to defend and protect myself, and heard the door keys (which were my safety line) jangle as they slid across the long bar top. With stools and ashtrays flying and tumbling around me, I felt my glasses fly off my face and heard them hit the floor just about the same time he pinned me down. *Are you kidding me, God? Again... really? This is rape number four! Oh, please, GOD, let me survive...*

After what seemed an eternity, he lifted me by my hair to steal even more power from me. Through my begging and pleading that I couldn't leave my nearly two-year-old son motherless, I somehow managed to convince him not to sodomize me or follow through with his threats to kill me. I was now trying to rationalize with an irrational and drugged person. *Why didn't I listen to my gut a little while ago? I KNEW when he made that "God" comment earlier that something was wrong. Why didn't I listen???*

Holding me by what little hair I had left, he dragged me to the cash registers and demanded all of the money, smashing my head into each one with each word. Some blows I braced myself from receiving – others I did not. *Am I really going to die tonight? Is my son really going to grow up without a mom? Why can't I reach him to scratch his eyes out or kick him, or even bite him? Why did I agree at the last minute to work the day after Christmas?*

After he got what he wanted, and a few more blows to my head accompanied by more threats of death, he ran out of the bar. My two regulars, who were outside waiting for me and drinking their six-pack as usual, never heard my screams penetrate the two very thick brick walls that separated us. *Now what? Where's my glasses? Where's the keys? Is he coming back in?*

I sat there on the floor for a few minutes, making sure he wasn't coming back, and scrambled to find my glasses and the keys. I went

70

over to the inner door, locked it, left the keys in the lock, and grabbed the phone. I called 911, my boss, and then my sleeping (now ex) husband to tell him I would be at the hospital because "something" happened at the bar. I got the answering machine. I went back to the inner door and stood there, with both hands on the keys, and felt my whole body shaking. It took the guidance of the four squads of police officers who showed up to convince me to turn the key.

Spending the next week in a daze, my mind unable to think or understand, not sleeping, not eating, and not feeling anything except the physical injuries that would take weeks to heal, I somehow made a snap decision to take my power back and not let him have *one more second* of power over me. I cannot explain what happened inside me, but I believe that after four assaults, at ages five, nine, fourteen, and twenty-eight, I was choosing to NO LONGER BE A VICTIM BUT A SURVIVOR!

This decision led to years of recovery, through individual and group therapy, reading spiritual and self-help books, and discovering a four-part questioning process that saved my life. I uncovered that I deeply needed to stop listening to my negative self-talk: my obsessive fears of his threat (that he would find and kill me when released from prison), and the thoughts of worthlessness, self-judgement, doubt, and depression that periodically appeared and almost led to my suicide two months after the assault.

It was also recovery from the deep sadness I carried after four assaults – my belief that I deserved them compounded by my verbally and emotionally abusive marriage, and the "victim" mentality that led me to give my power away for so many years. Even more important was the recovery from blaming myself because I had *not* trusted my instincts and prevented this last brutal attack. I was able to let go of the powerlessness I felt from the assaults directly, and the guilty feelings that maybe I wasn't processing the assaults in the way my therapists said I should be because I wasn't mistrusting the world around me. I was a woman who was surviving; I was in no way thriving. I was barely existing.

On the outside, you'd see a happy, joyful, peaceful Sue... and I really *was* happy, joyful, and peaceful on many levels. But on the inside, at a deep inner level, I was a mess. I was self-sabotaging my dreams and my future by continuing to engage in what I called my "mind chatter" that just would not let me rest in silence and move forward. I listened too intently and bought in to what that chatter had to say... and it nearly destroyed me.

I learned through those painful periods of transformation and healing, which were scattered far apart, that I had the power to CHOOSE what I would feel and believe. I had the power to BELIEVE that I was worthy and valuable, and could truly be the inspiring person so many people in my life told me I was. I had the power to EXPRESS *who I was* whenever I desired. I had the power to LET GO of the story of what I had believed defined ME.

Making these changes in my thought process was not an easy task... nor did it come without pain. But through that pain I discovered my "Truth Process," which ultimately allowed me at age fifty to step fully into *who I am* and be the visionary that I was always meant to be. Through this process I learned to put down the book of internal negativity that I was holding and no longer continue to read the same chapter over and over and over. I learned how to make the decision to shatter the illusions of my mind chatter, and find the recesses within that still held pockets of darkness and then shine a light so bright into those black holes that there was no place for that darkness to hide anymore.

Making that decision was born from my "Truth Process," whereby I often asked myself deeper questions – some positive and some not so positive. But I feel the most critical questions that surfaced were "Why aren't you a mistrusting and hate-filled person who is suspicious and afraid?" and "Why are you so willing to be vulnerable to others and let them see your light, even when you don't believe that you even have a light to shine?" And the only answers I could ever come up with were that I had a deeper trust inside that I had been aware of since the age

72

of four that revealed to me that *all* of my experiences, good and bad, were part of my reason for coming into this body at this particular point in time.

It was my soul contract with God to experience these events in order to further my evolution in a way I wouldn't always be able to see, but would be guided to understand as time marched forward.

Although I didn't trust my instinct that night, or on the other three occasions due to the fear that I was misjudging or being too suspicious of those men, I *did* trust the deeper awareness that there was a gift in this for me that I would see at some point. I know that may be very difficult for some people to understand, but that's how I felt deep inside. Some of you reading this might be wondering, "How can you call being brutally attacked a gift?" and, I admit, it wasn't easy… at first. But then I began to feel differently about myself and the attacks as I started to see the experiences through a different lens. The attacks ultimately became some of the greatest gifts of my life.

The most precious gift I received while sitting on the witness stand during my attacker's trial was that I KNEW the truth, and no matter how the defense attorney attempted to make me out to be a liar, I was strong and capable and sticking to the truth as I knew it to be. And *that* was a strength that others had said they had seen in me for years but *I had never felt* inside before. Now I did – fully and completely, and *no one* could *ever* take that away from me again – unless I CHOSE to give it away.

This was the beginning of my putting into action all of the tools and skills I had learned through the years of coping. This was the beginning of my learning to love myself and starting to really heal. This was the beginning of my willingness to reach out to others in a grander way than I had before in order to be that guide and mirror for them as they learned to envision a life they only dreamed about. This was the beginning and birth of the real ME.

The *real* ME learned to listen to and TRUST my intuition and my budding deeper belief in myself. It's really a matter of TRUST – trusting that niggling thought inside your head (even if you don't believe it) that says you *are* worthy and valuable – for truly, you are. It's a matter of trust that you recognize that you are not a victim of anything, but a survivor who hasn't learned how to thrive... yet. It's simply a matter of trust that you can put that book down and stop reading the same chapter, and that you *can* rise above your negative experiences, no matter how traumatic they may be. It's simply a matter of trust that you and I are here dancing this dance of life together, and that *we* can choose the music to dance to.

Turn it up and put your dancing shoes on! It's a beautiful song.

Susan L. Dascenzi, MSW, LCSW, is the CEO/Founder of True Visionaries, Inc., a heart-centered organization assisting those who want to quiet that negative internal voice through emotional mastery and freedom. An emotion/vision coach, licensed psychotherapist, author, and speaker for nearly twenty years, she's helped thousands of clients hone in on their core issues and facilitate change through her compassion, empathy, warmth, and humor. Get her four-part "Truth Process" and monthly ezine, *The Emotional Freedom Flight,* at www. SusanDascenzi.com.

The Magic of Letting Go: Intention, Attention, No Intention

Marci Shimoff

FOR THE FIRST THIRTY-SIX YEARS OF MY LIFE, I had been very achievement-driven. I worked hard, pushed myself, and was crystal clear about what I wanted. But, I wasn't very good at letting go, relaxing, and opening to receive what the universe brought me.

Early in my career, I'd learned a wonderful formula for manifesting anything in life from Bill Levacy, one of my life coaches. The formula consists of three rhyming steps:

Intention: Be very clear about what you want.

Attention: Focus your attention on what you desire. Make sure your thoughts, words, feelings and your actions are in alignment with your intention.

No tension: Relax, let go, be in a state of ease, and open to receive from the universe.

While I was really good at those first two steps – intention and attention – I had a hard time with the "no tension" step, even though the most wonderful miracles have come to me when I've been able to let go into "no tension." Perhaps the most dramatic example of this relates to my biggest career breakthrough. Let me share the story with you.

I was thirteen when I attended my first event featuring an inspirational speaker, Zig Ziglar. As I saw him walking the stage, passionately giving his speech and moving the entire audience, I said to myself, "That's what I'm supposed to do here on this planet." I had a very clear intention and vision. I saw myself traveling around the world inspiring millions of people to live their best lives possible. At that young age, my intention was clearly set.

My attention was also strong. For years, I did everything I could to support that intention happening. Eventually, I got an MBA in training and development (the closest degree I could find to match my intention), started my career as a corporate training consultant, and taught seminars on stress management and communication skills in Fortune 500 companies across the United States. I read every self-help book I found, attended every self-help seminar I could, studied other speakers' delivery styles, learned every self-development technique out there and followed the success principles I'd discovered in order to make my dream a reality.

I was fortunate to have an amazing mentor in Jack Canfield – years before the *Chicken Soup for the Soul* books had even been conceived. He taught me (and many others) how to deliver self-esteem training programs. Soon after I attended his "Train the Trainer" course, I began teaching those programs to women's audiences. Though I was having some success working for a seminar company teaching one-day training programs, I was frustrated because I wasn't having the big success I'd dreamed of.

On top of that, I was exhausted. I felt like a road warrior, traveling 200 days a year. I would speak all day long (in high heels), then get in a car at 5:30pm and drive three to four hours to the next city, fall fast asleep, and wake up early the next morning so I could be in the training room by 7:00am ready to do that routine all over again. I did that day in and day out.

And while I knew in my heart that inspiring people was what I was supposed to be doing, I sensed that there was something bigger that was supposed to happen. My vision was to reach more people worldwide, but I couldn't seem to break through to the next level in my career. I'd hit a wall.

Tired, confused, and drained, I started doubting my future: *What was next and how could I get there?*

As grace would have it, my dear friend, Janet Atwood, took me by the hand one day and said, "Marci, you're coming with me. You're burned out. You need a break. We're going on a seven-day silent meditation retreat." Shocked, I answered, "No way. I haven't been silent for more than two hours in my life! I can't imagine seven days of silence. Impossible." But Janet was insistent, so off we went to a week of what I thought would be silent torture.

The first few days were really challenging, but I finally settled in to the silence and started enjoying the ease that came with it. On the fourth day, in the middle of a meditation, a light bulb went on in my head, and I saw the words *Chicken Soup for the Woman's Soul.* As soon as I had that vision, I knew exactly what I was to do next – write that book.

At the time, only the original *Chicken Soup for the Soul* book had been published and nobody had thought of creating other specialty books. I just knew this was it – something that would touch many people and that was a calling for me! This was, I felt, a gift from the universe.

The only problem with the scenario was that I still had three more days of my silent retreat left. I'd just had the great epiphany of my life and I couldn't tell anybody!

So, as soon as the silence was over, I ran to the closest pay phone, called up Jack and said, "Listen to this: *Chicken Soup for the* Woman's *Soul.*" He said, "What a great idea! I can't believe nobody's thought of this before." He then called his publisher and said, "*Chicken Soup for the Woman's Soul.*" To which the publisher replied, "What a great idea. I can't believe nobody thought of that."

Within a few months I had a signed contract to co-author the book with Jack, Mark Victor Hansen, and my business partner, Jennifer Hawthorne. A year and a half later, *Chicken Soup for the Woman's Soul* was released and in its first week, hit #1 on the *New York Times* bestseller list. Since then, I've written a total of nine books that have sold fifteen million copies in thirty-three languages, and I've travelled around the world speaking about the messages in those books.

Relaxing into a deep state inside – the state of no tension – is what led to that pivotal "A-ha!" moment that transformed my career. It was proof to me that it's those three steps – intention, attention, and no tension – *together* that create magic in our lives.

Working on *Chicken Soup for the Woman's Soul* was more fulfilling than anything I'd ever done before in my career, as it was birthed out of pure inspiration. I could feel that I was moving in tune with the universe – that I had plugged into something bigger than me; I had just gotten on the train, and it was moving me forward.

After the book came out, I was quickly speaking to audiences 100 times bigger than those I was used to speaking to – I was reaching 10,000 people instead of 100 people at an event. And the best part was feeling like I was fulfilling my life purpose.

As time went on, I met amazing teachers who had been my idols in the transformational field. They were becoming my colleagues and friends, and I felt more empowered and more deeply fulfilled. I was getting to play in a bigger way.

Life After *Chicken Soup*

After I finished my seventh *Chicken Soup* book in seven years, I knew it was time to move on. I was burned out again. I was full of *Chicken Soup.* I'd lost the excitement and joy, and I sensed there was something else ahead for me. Remembering the magic formula, I decided it was time for another relaxation, ease cycle. I felt a pull toward deep inner reflection.

I believe we each have cycles in life — very active, outward cycles and then quieter, inward times. I had just completed an extremely active cycle, and I was craving some time to relax and go inside.

It wasn't easy for me to honor that desire to take it easy. Growing up, I always felt I had to stay busy, to be in constant motion. And certainly that feeling was reinforced by living in a society that focuses heavily on the outer cycle and doesn't tend to respect the power of the inner cycle.

But I'd gotten such a major lesson in the power of relaxing, that whenever I felt guilty about taking some time off, I quickly remembered the good that came out of it.

So, I took time off and did some soul searching: *What did I want to do next in my career?* I realized that I wanted to focus on happiness — researching the subject and finding out how people could experience greater happiness from the inside out. This was something I wanted and that I wanted to be able to share with others. (As the old saying goes, we teach what we most want to learn.)

After beginning the book, I went away on another silent meditation retreat to come up with the book title — this time I decided on a four-day retreat. (I figured that my *Chicken Soup* epiphany had come on the fourth day of my earlier week-long retreat, so I'd be efficient and give this one just four days.)

During the first three days of the retreat, while I wrote down more than 200 title ideas, none of them really excited me. But sure enough, during my meditation on the fourth morning, the title *Happy for No Reason* came to me, and I knew that was the next book. It described exactly the type of happiness that I was exploring and writing about. Once again, I felt the universe had delivered a beautiful gift.

That book was truly a work of my heart. I learned so much in the process of writing the book — and I became much happier by applying what I learned. It worked.

Once *Happy for No Reason* was out in the world, I did some more soul-searching, and it became clear to me that the next book I wanted to write was about unconditional love, the kind of love that doesn't depend on a person, situation, or romantic partner – the love that is our essence. That's how my ninth book, *Love for No Reason,* was born. It feels as though this book, too, had been conceived from inspiration.

I'm thrilled that both of these books also became *New York Times* bestsellers and that their messages of unconditional love and happiness have reached many people around the world. This is further proof that when I relax and let the universe flow through me, the benefits are infinitely more profound.

Tips for No Tension

These days, whenever I feel out of balance or stuck, I lean into that "no tension" step of my magic formula. That's what puts me back into the flow of creativity and love.

Since the art of letting go is still something I haven't mastered, I think of three words that help remind me how to relax into no tension. Perhaps they'll help you:

The first word is "trust." Trust yourself and trust life. Ask, *"What can I do to move into that state of ease? What's the next step for me? What expands me?"* Then trust your inner voice to move in that direction.

The second word is "courage." Have the courage to hang in there, get through the difficult times, and keep moving forward. No matter what it looks like on the outside, listen to your heart and have the courage to follow it.

The third word is "compassion." We need compassion, particularly with ourselves. Remember, in the midst of whatever challenge you may be facing, offer yourself care and understanding. Nurture and nourish yourself. You'll be able to get through anything if you can be gentle, loving, and compassionate with yourself.

People often ask me if taking care of themselves and focusing on their own inner happiness and love is selfish. Absolutely not. On the contrary, I believe it's the least selfish thing that you can do. The more fulfilled you are, the more you're able to offer to the world. The world gets the benefit of your elevated energy.

That concept is reflected beautifully in my favorite Chinese proverb:

When there is light in the soul, there will be beauty in the person.
When there is beauty in the person, there will be harmony in the house.
When there is harmony in the house, there will be order in the nation.
And when there is order in the nation, there will be peace in the world.

My wish you for you is that you feel the love in your heart and the light in your soul. May we each experience that love and light so we can light up and transform this world.

Marci Shimoff is a #1 *New York Times* bestselling author, a world-renowned transformational teacher, and an expert on happiness, success, and unconditional love. Marci's books include the *New York Times* bestsellers, **Love for No Reason, Happy for No Reason,** and six titles in the phenomenally successful **Chicken Soup for the Woman's Soul** series. Her books have sold more than fifteen million copies worldwide in thirty-three languages. Marci is also a featured teacher in the international film and book sensation, *The Secret.* Visit her website at www.HappyForNoReason.com.

The Magic of Misty

Diane Jackson, MFT

"Until he extends the circle of his compassion to all living things,
man will not himself find peace."
– Albert Schweitzer

ANIMALS POSSESS THE LOVING ENERGY to not only enrich our lives but transform them. Seeing them with our hearts instead of just with our eyes provides an opportunity to delve deeper into our own humanity. When we live with open and loving hearts, we can honor the divinity of all life, recognizing that each life has meaning and purpose, and holds tremendous value. Having respectful and responsible relationships, whether they are with other humans, mammals, birds, reptiles, fish, or insects, is honoring the interconnectedness of all life on the planet, whether we understand it or not.

Gifts from an Angel

My mother, due to her own life circumstances and personal challenges, pulled away from me when I was three. She retreated into her own private world and began drinking as a way of coping and escaping reality. Unable to properly care for herself, let alone me, this is when I became her caretaker. Too young to understand the unrealistic magnitude of the role, I often felt unsure of myself, frightened, embarrassed, and alone. As much as I loved her and knew she loved me, in my heart the fact remained that she wasn't able to be there for me and I couldn't count on her to look after me.

Divinely timed, that same year she placed a box under our Christmas tree. With festive Christmas music playing in the background and under twinkling lights and tinsel, the most amazing angel peered out of that box. She couldn't fly and didn't have wings, but rather four paws, a wet nose, warm kisses, and big brown eyes that were full of love. This angel of mine was a beautiful Sheltie puppy. I named this bundle of energy and fur Misty.

Misty and I lived in the midst of a family that was perpetually in emotional crisis. There were always plenty of waves of drama, and being at the effect of the waves often left me feeling emotionally nauseous. With the unspoken expectation that I would just be good and take care of myself, I knew that my family wasn't capable of attending to my needs. So I set out to not need much and to not make any waves of my own. Survival meant that I learned to live with a smile on my face, pretending to be strong even though I often felt unsure of myself and scared. Relief came when I was alone with Misty, because in her presence I could just be myself. She simply loved me for me and accepted me unconditionally.

While my grandfather was away at work, my mother and grandmother would frequently engage in marathon yelling escapades. They were often unaware of where I was hiding: in my safe place down under the avocado tree with Misty by my side. Under that tree the yelling could still be heard, and with each loud word and sound I could see her concern and feel my own. She and I would hold steady and pause, listening for what would come next. Leaning into her soft fur I felt safe and loved, and with my arms wrapped firmly around her I knew she felt the same. When I would quietly cry, Misty would work her magic and tend to my hurting heart with the gift of her love. She would give me the gentlest licks of reassurance and then gaze deeply into my eyes and really see ME! In those moments I knew I was valuable, worthy, and deeply loved. She got me through some very dark moments, days, and years, and the bond between us was healing salve for my aching heart.

Misty taught me a lot about life and myself. She seemed to naturally embody qualities of a mother. She was always miraculously there for me when I needed her, displaying amazing grace, and through her calm and steady actions she taught me patience, acceptance, kindness, gentleness, and love. It was because of Misty's unwavering unconditional love that my heart learned about safety and trust.

All the other animals around our home felt safe and trusted her as well. When Charlotte, my pet chicken, wasn't hitching a ride on my shoulder, I would frequently put her on Misty's back and ask them to accompany me around the property. We encountered bugs of all sorts living out their lives and were on the lookout for any other critters to engage with in play. Whenever some being crossed our path, Misty would pause and observe with curiosity. Once when Henrietta, another pet chicken of mine, led her baby chicks out of the shed and into the yard for the first time, Misty just sat and observed the newest additions with motherly attentiveness. In her relationship with me as well as in her interactions with nature and the other animals, she allowed me to see with a wider lens the value of cultivating inherent respect and reverence for all life.

Lessons Learned

The magic of Misty was her capacity to simply love all beings. She kept her heart open while suffering alongside me, offering love and forgiveness rather than anger and hostility. Knowing in my heart the pureness and truth in her actions, I tried to follow in her paw prints, working hard to emulate that kind of acceptance of the human condition and of my family, and in particular my mother's personal limitations.

Missing parental guidance and having to figure out the world by myself, I grew up very quickly. Yet like many teens I thought I knew more than I did. I wanted so badly to escape the destructive and toxic relationship of my grandmother and mother that I didn't see the path that I was on. I was walking myself right into the arms of an extremely abusive, older, sociopathic man. However, it was because of this relationship that I met a remarkable being. She was a beautiful and elegant Doberman named Anaconda, and she supported me through the darkest landscape of domestic violence and kept my spirit alive.

All the signs were there of mistreatment if I had just paid attention. Mixed in with the kindness this man offered her was blatant abuse. Although I saw it at the time, just knowing he was capable of such destructive behavior kept me stuck in the throes of gripping fear. Rather than listen to my intuition and advocate for her and myself, my own terror allowed me to dismiss it away. I went into a pretend mode, hoping it would get better. It didn't, and still I didn't listen. It is no exaggeration to say he continually tortured her and me for a number of years. The price paid for not listening to me and not advocating for her was quite heavy. What kept me going forward was the light and sparkle in her eyes. She beamed love my way and it kept breathing life into my soul.

While I didn't listen to my inner voice, I did pay attention to her. Despite how she was treated by him, she walked this earth with her head held high, claiming her power with each step. She didn't let him take that away from her. Her presence in my life was the constant mirror to the divinity that resided within me. In her strength and power she invited me to find my own power and she lovingly bolstered my courage. With all that display of strength, she also shared her gentle, sensitive, and playful side, which allowed me to stay true to my own compassionate heart. Finally, after assessing our level of danger, I stepped up and claimed me, rescued her, and together we bravely moved forward on life's path. My journey out of that unbelievable nightmare was because of the safety she created and her all-encompassing love of me.

There isn't any point in my life where the presence and love of an animal hasn't been there, and despite my life circumstances, animals have always reminded me to stay connected to the truth of my heart and soul. In their expression of unconditional love, they have held me securely on life's path when conditions threatened to knock me down and out. The resilience of my mind, body, and spirit has been fueled by the love and grace of the animals that have walked life's journey with me. I am profoundly grateful that their love allowed me to keep my heart open to live life with compassion and empathy.

Walling off your heart from others just because some individuals have treated you badly doesn't keep you safe; it imprisons you in a state of anger and ultimately fear. If you are willing to pause and pay attention then you can see that animals are teachers in the language of love. Attuning to their hearts can give us a deeper appreciation for our own experience. They illuminate the capacity for us to give and receive love, teach us how to be in the present moment, and remind us to play, laugh, and be joyful. In their kind and patient way they teach us that it is about continually showing up to the possibilities of life, never giving up who we are, and honoring the connection with the wonderful and mysterious spirit of the divine. Providing children with opportunities to value, respect, and love animals and nature as part of the world they live in provides them with a lifelong connection to energy and love. Animals are masterful teachers and healers of the heart. All they need is a chance to make an impression on our hearts and we as the human race are better for it.

I live with a grateful heart that I was so blessed to meet Misty at such a young age, for she gave me the resilience, courage, fortitude, and energy to carry on. She saw my inner light and added her own beautiful glow to propel me forward. She instilled hope when many days looked bleak. The powerful impact this divine four-legged being had on my heart and life altered me forever. My experiences with Misty inspired me to live with my heart open, appreciating and respecting all animals and beings equally. I recognized early on that we all live on this magnificent planet – just in different bodies, and that just because animals speak in a language that humans don't readily understand doesn't mean they don't need our love and support. They are fellow souls travelling this earth with us. I am, and will always be, grateful that a dear and magical soul named Misty came into my life and left paw prints on my heart forever.

"Be kind, be gentle, be patient, forgive, and act with
compassion for all beings."
– Misty and Diane

My Hope

My hope in sharing my experience with Misty is that it has inspired you to see the graceful power of an animal's love. If you have ever wondered about bringing an animal into your life, or if a loved animal has passed and your heart feels nudged to explore the possibility of bringing another one into it, then I encourage you to go within and imagine the love and connection that can be available to you in that relationship. It will truly be like no other. So many amazing animals are waiting for a human to connect with them. Whether it is a young, energetic being; a middle-aged being; or a wise, senior one, it will offer you a grateful heart and a playful spirit. There is so much support, joy, and nourishment awaiting you if you choose to share your life's path with an animal. You will make a difference in each other's lives. If you are willing to look deep into your own animal's eyes you will see your own magnificence. So I invite you to let this magical love come into your heart and transform your life.

Diane Jackson is a licensed marriage family therapist and the co-founder of a non-profit animal sanctuary, Peace For All Animals. A lifelong advocate for the humane treatment of humans and animals, Diane focuses on the human/animal bond and the transformative power of that relationship. She is committed to inspiring people to act with greater levels of compassion for all beings. Visit Diane at www.PeaceForAllAnimals.org to learn more about her and her work.

Intuitively Speaking: Learning to Listen to My Inner Voice

Melinda Kapor

"Intuition is a spiritual faculty and does not explain,
but simply points the way."
– Florence Scovel Shinn

IRRITATED, MY DATE LEANED OVER in the front seat of his car and bit me hard on the lip, causing it to bleed. I had agreed to go out with him even though we'd only just met during my lunch break. As evening drew near, however, I *intuitively* felt that I didn't want him to see where I lived. "Pick me up on the corner of Hyde and Pacific," I told him.

"I'm taking you home with me," he said as we drove off. Yet when he stopped at a light on a one-way street, I *instinctively* jumped out and ran the other way, catching a cable car to get home and saving myself, I am sure, from further injury.

This experience of mine, as a young woman living in San Francisco, demonstrates the subtle difference between instinct and intuition. While very similar and often referred to interchangeably, instinct is more basic, more animalistic – sort of an ingrained self-preservation. Intuition, on the other hand, is an inner knowing.

We're all born with elemental instinct. It's as much a part of us as breathing – natural without thought, protecting us from harm. When a young child refuses to eat, for example, it's often because the child instinctively knows not to. My baby son invariably was coming down with some ailment whenever he refused to eat.

Ordering halibut once in a California restaurant, a Pacific fish that I loved, I had the strong sense after one bite not to eat it. But I was an invited guest, and not wanting to be rude, I ate the fish. Within twenty minutes I had a severe case of hives, from my knees down, that lasted two weeks. This wasn't the first time I had had such a feeling regarding certain foods with negative consequences, but it certainly was the most serious. I learned the hard way to listen to my instincts.

> *"The intuitive mind is a sacred gift and the*
> *rational mind is a faithful servant.*
> *We have created a society that honors the servant*
> *and has forgotten the gift."*
> *– Albert Einstein*

While I think of instinct as more of an innate means of survival, intuition is our link to the Divine, to The Source, to God. It's our Higher Self, Guardian Angel, Inner Voice, even gut feeling – whatever term one feels comfortable using. Our intuition comes through to protect and guide, always and in all ways, for the Higher Good of those involved.

For some people intuition comes easily; others have to work on developing it. Youngsters are apt to be intuitive prior to going to school, before logical thought is encouraged as the way to arrive at a conclusion. Using the powerful combination of intuition and intellect is not taught in typical educational systems. Fortunately, fostering intuition is something we can work on ourselves; the more we recognize and honor our own, the more it will evolve to serve us.

"Intuition doesn't always present itself as a knowing;
sometimes it speaks, even shouts for attention."
— *Melinda Kapor*

In the early eighties, my Yugoslavian boyfriend asked me to meet him in Paris where he was going for a month to work. I thought, "Why not?" I was between jobs and had already made a decision to live elsewhere than my home state. I'd even considered living in Europe, but had no idea how to make that a reality. With his invitation to Paris, my lover became not the reason for moving, but the catalyst for living abroad. I wanted to live my life fully, not read longingly about someone else's adventures. I sold my car, packed my bag, and left.

Paris was wonderful, but I didn't want to stay there after my flame returned to his country. Where to go? As an American, it would have been impossible to find work in Yugoslavia at the time. I felt I would like the Mediterranean culture of Italy, though I'd never been there, and was particularly drawn to Rome. On one of my last nights in Paris, my destination was confirmed when I dreamt of a voice that said, "Go to Rome."

I soon left Paris for Rome by train, taking a detour to Zurich en route to visit a college friend. After a couple of days, I decided to continue my journey, choosing to save on hotel costs by traveling at night. I went to the train station and bought a first class ticket to Rome — more comfortable and safer, I thought, than second class would be.

The train cars were separated into individual compartments, one after another, each with six seats, three facing three. Naively I sat in an empty compartment, taking a seat by the window. I remember vividly how I was dressed: jeans, a teal-blue turtleneck, my long hair pulled away from my face with a rubber band, and little makeup.

I'd just settled into my seat when a heavy, pox-faced man came into the compartment and sat across from me. My heart immediately started to race and straightaway I didn't like him. "Get out of here!" an inner voice urged, but I responded, as if discussing it, "Don't be silly."

The man said he knew I was from California by my accent. He was Swiss and traveling to Chiasso on the Italian border, three hours away.

I rose to throw away my coffee cup outside the compartment. "Throw it here," he said, indicating the waste bin under the window. Then, as I opened my *Time* magazine, he turned on my seat's overhead lamp, saying, "This is better for reading," simultaneously switching off the brighter, main light. These were ploys, I later realized, to control the situation.

An inner voice screamed, "Get out! Get out of here now!" But still I stayed, rationalizing that my bag was heavy and hard to move. All I had to do, I thought, was stay awake until he got off.

With his trying to engage me in conversation, I told him, "Please, I just want to read." "Okay," he replied, opening his briefcase as I looked down at my magazine. "Read this," he said and handed me a photocopy of a Boston newspaper article. "It's for you," he smiled, with his entwined hands resting on his paunch, his slit-like eyes gleaming. I read the headline: "Man Accused of Rape."

Jumping up I exclaimed, "I don't want to be near you," but before I could open the sliding door of the compartment, he leapt up and struck me hard on the face, hitting my left ear and upper cheek. (My ear rang from the blow for days.)

The conductor had just passed a few minutes before to check our tickets, closing the door behind him before moving on. "He hit me! He hit me!" I screamed as I jerked the door back open, drawing everyone's attention. The conductor returned and the passengers of other compartments all stuck their heads into the corridor to see what the noise was about.

The man started to yell in English, using filthy language, saying that I had teased him and led him on. Then he started to presumably reiterate the same in German. The conductor insisted that the ranting man move to another car, several away from ours. Terrified and shaken, I moved into the compartment adjacent to mine where five of the six seats were taken. I sat in the one vacant middle seat and burst into tears.

The kind man to my right was a college professor from Rome who spoke English. He was astounded that I was going to a city where I knew no one – young Italian women at that time would never do such a thing – and handed me his card, saying to call him should I need help.

At midnight we rolled into the Chiasso train station, the destination of my assailant. When he descended from the train, he didn't exit with the other passengers, but hid behind a partition, peeking around the corner until he saw where I was. Coming over to my compartment window to yell obscenities at me, he found himself instead facing the professor, who stood there as a protective barrier. Furious, the man cursed him. As the train started to pull out of the station, the professor gave him an explicit reply.

Shortly after, the professor followed through on his earlier suggestion that I get a *cuccette,* or bed, in a sleeping car, since we wouldn't arrive in Rome until 9:00am. A conductor whom he asked found one for me. After thanking the kind professor and saying good-bye, I was accompanied to where I would spend the night.

No matter how traumatic this episode on the train was, it also greatly benefitted me. Consequently I arrived in Rome more cautious than I would have been otherwise. Apart from the professor, I knew no one and my lack of the language made relying on my intuition all the more essential. Whether it actually spoke to me or not, I had learned to listen to my inner voice and trusted it would guide me true.

Several years later, a *knowing* led me to Milan. I said it was for work, but the real reason was I *felt* I needed to be there. During the first month after my move, I met the man who would become my husband.

"You get your intuition back when you make space for it, when you stop the chattering of the rational mind."
— Anne Lamott

Sometimes I'm so wrought with options that I get caught in a swirling whirlpool of ideas. These are times that I have to take a breath, let it go, and allow the answer to come. For some people meditation helps to get to that place of knowing. For others it can be as simple as clearing the mind with methodical, physical activity, allowing room for intuition to flourish.

I still have to work on being a good listener to my intuitive self. Like the game where players take two steps forward, one step back, I go backwards when my mind takes over with ricocheting thoughts. But, as in a game, it's my overall advancement that counts in the end.

Last year, while searching for a new apartment, I had an immediate knowing that I'd found it upon walking into an airy place on the eighth floor of a ten-story building. Still I belabored over the decision, thinking and rethinking about the pros and cons. It didn't have everything we were looking for, yet it offered so much more. While rushing around, continuing to see other options, my inner voice finally matter-of-factly said, "I gave you a sign; why do you doubt?"

"You're right," I thought, laughing to myself. Should I not listen to my *intuition* speak, it will raise its voice to be *heard*.

We moved into the apartment shortly after. If an intuition can smile, mine surely did.

A native Californian, **Melinda Kapor** never thought she would leave her home state, but her first trip overseas to Dubrovnik, then part of Yugoslavia, in the early 1980s, changed everything. Just fourteen months later she was living in Italy, where she still resides today. With a degree in sociology from UC Berkeley, Melinda is an intercultural consultant, writer, and eclectic explorer of life. To learn more visit www.MelindaKapor.com.

Dream Your Dance,
Dance Your Dream

Katya, MSSW, Minister of Spiritual Peacemaking

EVERYONE I WAS CARING FOR WAS PREPARING to go Home, but somehow I knew that when the time is right, your soul mate appears. What you are looking for is looking for you.

It was my first day back at work as a hospice social worker after six weeks of confinement and bed rest due to an automobile accident. I'd been rear-ended and the effects of the spinal injury were seemingly minimal, however I was placed in the hospice unit at the hospital rather than driving all over the county to counsel and support patients and their families. As I made my rounds, I heard classical guitar music wafting through the unit. Pausing at the door to observe the family dynamics of Carol, the patient in 9B, I clearly heard a voice say to me, "There's your husband." Stunned by the audaciousness of the comment, I quietly responded, "Are you serious? Get REAL!!!" and entered the room to meet with the family. Having read the chart, and aware of those present, I observed the scenario of Randy, the guitarist, sitting at the foot of the bed, while the other son, Allen, closely adjacent to the bedside, had his feet resting next to his mother's, holding her hand. Their eyes were closed and I sensed a connection of intimacy between them that suggested they were off together somewhere in time.

My entrance created an interruption in the music and despite my efforts to calm the anxiety of the music maker, Randy insisted that his older brother awaken and join him in the discussion about their mother. The garden was the only available place to talk and as we walked there I noticed the elder son reluctantly lingering behind. I observed that his body was slowly making its way, however his spirit seemed preoccupied and had not caught up with the busyness of the earthly affairs. I briefly explained my position on the staff and began answering the numerous queries fired at me by Randy. I suggested that it was time to thank, bless, and release their mother (in their own words) so that she could feel their permission to get on with her journey.

In that moment, Allen raised his head, opened his eyes, and joined us like he had just experienced a moment of communion. His spirit, united to Carol's, had popped back, united with mine, and the union was blessed on earth as in heaven. Little did I know that Carol had added an addendum to her will only twenty days prior that Allen be given his grandmother's ring with the message, "This is for your new bride."

Allen and I had known each other five days when he proposed and fifteen days total when we had our wedding ceremony, blessing each other, Mother Earth, our families, and friends on New Year's morning under a new, blue, full moon.

We lived all over the country when Allen, a gifted medical architect, who had worked for all of the "Big-Boys," was finally brought to Rochester, New York, as managing partner of a firm to design a cancer research treatment center for the King of Jordan in Amman. Three and a half months after our arrival and I was still unpacking; Allen returned home from a trip to Boston complaining of pains in his lower back. When a hot bath and massage didn't help and he began passing blood clots the size of chicken livers from a place where men only want fluids to flow, it was off to the big teaching hospital. Five and a half hours later, we were sent home with an antibiotic and a directive to call the urology department in three weeks. Pushing himself to go to work the next morning, Allen secured the contact of a urologist from one of the partners in the firm. We were in his office the next day at 2:30am.

The game was on. Weeks later, after several visits with various doctors, numerous blood draws to pathology, and stays in two hospitals, Allen was diagnosed with stage four urothelial cancer. The treatments for this vigorous and aggressive disease were twenty-five years old because of its rarity and lack of funding for research and updates.

A courageous trooper, Allen faced surgery, chemotherapy, and radiation with unflinching nerve and determination while I supported him as caretaker, nurse, social worker, minister, and spouse in a new city with no family or friends. I jumped back into the health-care system after seventeen years, only to find that we had regressed, I think, in part due to the overwhelming numbers needing care.

I made contact with a urologist/oncologist in Colorado where we had lived who practiced complementary medicine. She decided to direct me in caring for Allen holistically as his practitioner and she would guide me due to my knowledge and experience. I did shamanic work, prayer work, and connected with every spiritual group I could think of as I was now an ordained Minister of Spiritual Peacemaking honoring all the different traditions.

Changing dressings under sterilized conditions for the nephrostomy tube in his right kidney, monitoring his diet, figuring out how to clear the effects of the poisonous chemotherapy drugs from his palate so he could get nourishment, was my daily practice, while detoxing his body, as the chemo only works for twenty-four to forty-eight hours. It has such a horrific effect breaking down the rest of the body, while efforts were made to shrink the tumor that was growing exponentially fast in my beloved's gut. All these Herculean efforts, securing audio tapes, and supporting his inner work while I dealt with attorneys, insurance companies, and bureaucratic paper shuffling ad nauseam. I was dancing as fast as I could and some days it just wasn't fast enough.

Allen had been professionally raped by the firm that had brought us to Rochester. They had stolen his portfolio and research of thirty-five years, and in the heavily regulated state of New York I was told by a lawyer, "Pick your battles. A fight in the courts would kill him for sure."

Stripped of everything except our insurance, we continued to forge ahead. Allen was emasculated in a seven-and-a-half-hour surgery that was supposed to last eleven hours. "What were you up to?" was the query I was greeted with when the doctors arrived to speak with me. They couldn't find the massive tumor, there was no bleeding, and twenty-nine lymph nodes were removed and sent to pathology, and they couldn't find any cancer. I questioned why they hadn't called me as they had at the end of the procedure to ask what I wanted them to do. "Take a wait and see before you strip his pelvis," would have been my answer as Allen and I had prayed for a miracle.

Allen was out searching for a new job six weeks later and found two; one in Sacramento, California, and the other in North Carolina. It was 2008, the banks went belly up as the dark economic shadow was sweeping the country, and everyone pulled back. Allen had his arthritic hip replaced and continued to work to finish off the lower level of our home while we waited to see how the world would recover from the financial crisis.

Allen had initially asked me to divorce him after the surgery, but knowing this was a pop quiz, I told him, "I'll find nine hundred and ninety-nine other ways to love you. I'm in this for the long haul." We overcame every obstacle and hurdled every challenge to our passionate love for each other. Like horse and jockey riding the Kentucky Derby, we were one in spirit. We rounded the final turn and were headed for the home stretch when Allen was hit with yet another challenge. His former wife now wanted more money from his disability for child support for his three thirty-some-year-old adult children. He had paid upwards of $60,000, which continued two years beyond their full emancipation, and she wanted more. Lying to the courts, in a system that is overburdened and sees men as deadbeat dads, I listened to the judge condemn and crucify my beloved so he could wash his hands and be done with what he didn't want to be bothered with anymore.

The parallels of Pontius Pilate had resurfaced and the scourgings were too numerous to count. Allen had been professionally raped and abused, medically violated, and stripped of his manhood. He was lied to, dishonored, and vehemently and unconscionably humiliated in the courts as the judge wielded his sword. "I don't care if you die," was the lance that pierced Allen's side and his head hung from the crucifixion.

His contract was now finished.

How much can the human spirit endure? The cancer had now returned after eighteen months and there were no treatments and no money for out-of-pocket care.

"If Jesus can give up his life to his Father, so can I," said Allen on Good Friday after singing in the choir with me, skinny and bald. With a heart full of love for his God, for me, his children, and his music, his integrity was undamaged. A friend helped me take him to Florida to swim in the ocean, the second thing on his bucket list. The other item was to dance with me one more time, and this would have to be left in the hands of the Divine.

Allen transformed, transcended, and transpired on March 25th, and the following Wednesday in Holy Week was his memorial, preceded by a *ceilidh* at our home. By Easter Sunday, I didn't know the difference between Jesus and Allen. Giving up your life in love is how to live fully, and most fully when being crucified.

My beloved had been watched over, looked after, cared for, protected, and guided all the way Home. And he took me with him. Yes, we danced all the way like Fred and Ginger. "Heaven, I'm in heaven" were the words he sang to me, and that continues to support me in living after twenty-five years. A gentle giant, kind, loving, and a good and faithful servant who had served humanity with grace and dignity. "He was way ahead of his time. One of the finest architects the world has ever known, especially in the field of health care," were the words of his mentor and others who had worked with him. Allen is now working to help redesign our world.

He is one of my guardian angels among the troops who work with me. He has shown me there is no death. We simply transition to full spirit and keep going. Our loved ones are very present to us and only want to help. There are many being called as we need all the assistance we can receive for the healing work in the world. As life intensifies, we must rely on the fact that we are never alone. However, the caveat is, "They will not intrude. We must ASK for their help."

More and more individuals are being gifted to do the work of healing – raising the consciousness and lifting the fear. Our collective intelligence or "world mind" is unique in its capacity to interact at all levels. This "Oneness Mind" is seeking solutions as Spirit at an unimaginable rate and is unlocking a higher, more powerful system of operating within many who have awakened and answered the call to serve.

Say "YES" to Life. "YES" to love. And "YES" forever becomes your prayer. It puts you in sync with the flow to allow Spirit to breathe as you, always, in all ways. Nothing less will do. Nothing less will heal our world. Nothing less is life truly lived.

⌒⫯⌒

Breathed by Spirit, moving her through the "Dance," **Reverend Katya** has become a PROVOCATEUR of LIFE. As a motivational speaker, Playshop Facilitator, life coach, minister, and healer, she functions as God's Ambassadress guiding others to feel and know their authentic Self. www.RevKatya.com invites you to celebrate life in this "Dance of Spirit." This story is excerpted from her forthcoming book, *Born for Greatness: Live Your Essence.*

cᘰ⟶

Joy, Oneness, and Finding Courage on the Way Home

Tamee Knox-Polonski

Energy as Joy

THERE WAS NO WAY TO PREDICT WHAT would happen to me during the summer of 2006. Nothing gave me any clues about or words to describe the earth's profound energy that came my way that day. A divine electrical circuit to become one with expansion and a hidden magnificence captivated my attention like nothing before. The offering – a conscious spark as bright as the sun. It was as if Mother Earth, a battery of strength and electrical charges, produced her divine current which she generously chose to share with me and which stimulated me to be more alive. The manifestation was profound. It was a sound vibration in this dimension as "JOY" and caused a shaking of my blood so deep that it had the dominance to stop me and drop me forward towards the ground, grabbing my gut.

"What just happened?" I thought. "Who said that word?" I wondered. But in an instant my mind-chatter shut off and I felt an internal peace and quiet that I had never experienced before. I was still connected to the things around me. For example, I could see my children and where we were walking, but another part of me was in an etheric, blissful space, floating along in perfect harmony. A part of my mind/body connection that I had never even known existed just clicked into place. "Oh my, this IS JOY," I thought – not just a definition based on a past experience that created a laugh or a smile. Not a taught concept from a story or elder. This was JOY in its most intimate and innate state – so deep, rich, and internal that it could only come from Source, THE Source, Creator – the Divine birthplace referred to as home. Not only was I part of it in that moment, I was *aware* of it, a distinct realization that would change my life forever.

A Flashback to Where It Began

Instantly remembering that this wasn't the first time that Creator had shared its beauty with me, I flashed back to the spring of 1995. I was walking in a parking lot in California, and out of nowhere I heard a voice in my being say, "JOY." I giggled and a feeling of insane happiness filled me. It was an internal happiness that touched and penetrated layers of the self that I had never been introduced to before that moment. After that day my perception of life was with a deeper sensitivity and somewhat better understanding of its offerings and how precious each moment is.

The first transmission in 1995 was much more subtle and gentle than the one I speak of now. It was like a little friendly nudge or dash of cinnamon one adds to oatmeal to give it a certain fiery flavor. Nonetheless it was a needed gift to fuel me forward in my life. I can now answer the burning questions "Why are we here?" and "What is our purpose as humans?" knowing that what I was searching for was the purpose and passion of my existence. Although waking up each morning and accomplishing my many goals was rewarding, there was some deeper sense of me that knew I was not complete with what I was creating or taking in. There was a part that was just settling for what was.

Awareness and Courage

Although I wasn't exactly sure what was happening on all levels, I realized the biggest gift/gifting was that once these transmissions or transfers happened, this new consciousness was now part of me. It was a memory that I could pull up anytime and go to for reassurance in uncertain and chaotic times, just like a computer program works, or pulling up your favorite iTunes song. You think of it, connect it to your consciousness, and then get in touch with the energetics of it.

I soon found myself living through the memories at a deeper level. This was particularly helpful six weeks after the birth of my second child, when I became very weak and my body had a hard time reclaiming the strength it once had. My weight also fell dramatically during the first two years after her birth; I was very sleep-deprived and began questioning life more than living it. Inside of my mind and being things were not appealing, thoughts were not pleasing, and life in general was not engaging. There was so much good around me, but I wasn't fulfilled. Where was the pleasure? By remembering JOY, I was guided to explore forgiveness and let go of negativity. As I did, limiting judgments evaporated. I opened my mind to any and all possibilities. New energy was flowing through me and around me. I was changing fast.

Secretly I kept longing for those tiny moments of strength and beauty I'd experienced back in 1995 and 2006. Where were they hiding? Desperate for that sense of power, pleasure, and beauty again, I begged out loud, "Show me! Show me everything I need to know about Your love and the energy You gifted me in the spring of 1995 and summer of 2006. Trust me. I promise to respect it, and commit to the knowledge behind it." I waited... and waited... and waited some more. Five minutes passed and nothing happened. There I sat, in my silence, breathing deeply, with tears running down my face, knowing now that on some level that moment was probably more powerful than any energy surge I had previously had.

Then I thought, "Did I just say that? Am I praying?" I laughed at myself. I never wanted or had the need for anything like that before. I guess at that point I knew my life wasn't just changing anymore; it had already been altered. My consciousness had shifted.

That was the day I found the courage to say good-bye to ego as I knew it and hello to truth and self-realization. I began paying attention to my world in a very different way. It was as if an unusual force was nudging me this time, one that came up and through my body and dominated me and caused me to start making drastic changes in my life. I knew that with my new commitment to truth, things were not going to be easy for me and the ones who loved me. Change was imminent; more letting go and deeper reflection of self was needed. My soul's story was ready to unfold.

The Agreement

I began changing my life. I went from lifting weights to practicing yoga and breath-work; from no naps to learning the skillful art of self-rest, soothing, and meditation. My diet went from the typical "eat anything" to "filtered, free, and purified." Sour relationships slowly dissolved. My primary focus became energy and consciousness. Homeopathy, acupuncture, aromatherapy, herbs, past-life regression, tai chi, shamanism, Kabbalah, muscle-testing, nature, water, cell-level healing, sound vibration, and more were becoming a deeper part of my vocabulary, and their unique energies began filling the hole in my heart. I felt a richness and nourishment deep in my being. Each day I realized that I had so much to learn, so much to be grateful for, so much to discover. I also understood that it would be quite the challenge to keep my ego quiet and tucked away. The biggest lesson I learned was how limited and separate I had been from the truth of who we are as humans, divinity, and pure energy source.

No Turning Back

It was no mistake that I had had to be a student in those past years, because if I'd not prepared myself to receive the third transmission in the spring of 2010, what was about to happen would have overpowered me and caused tremendous shock to my body's system.

As previously, the energy came through as JOY. First came a gripping sensation in my navel. Then a full blast of electrical energy that bypassed every Law of Nature shot through me. I felt invincible, untouchable, and unbeatable. In that moment all challenges disappeared. For the next minute or two my strength increased, my body mass increased, and my overall energy increased consistently. I could feel a flow throughout my body that was not only oceanic, but as vast as the ocean. It was bigger and deeper than I. It reached far beyond my physical form and was compressed smaller and tighter than any molecular form. I could feel my blood pulsating and my lymphatic system flowing. There was joy, complete JOY, in every cell, organ, muscle fiber, synapse, and nerve ending. I focused on my breath and tried to stay as grounded as possible, paying most attention to the area around my navel, as this seemed to be the physical energetic source. The transmission lasted for about twenty-four to thirty-six hours, and then slowly started to dissipate. But again, I have the memory and awareness of it there, and to this day it lives in my cells and my mind/body matrix.

Oneness

The description of JOY and this strength is hard to put on paper, but the importance I share with you is that this energy is around us, surrounds us, lives inside us, IS us. It is where the stillness of the mind meets the stillness of a breath, and in that moment all creation can manifest. It visits us in many forms. Its blueprint is in nature. It shines in the plants, animals, food, and water. It vibrates in the sound of a musical note. It can take place just in walking. It is hidden in raindrops, the skin of an apple, a bird's chirp, the spaces between our teeth and bones. It is in the source of life that manifests as the physical form and beyond.

We are tapping in to it daily as creativity, love, movement, and breath. Other names for it are chi, zero point, no mind, *prana*, theta point, and ascension. It is there for us to explore and to guide us along the life path. Mindfulness is at the root of its energy. Your intention and questions stimulate the force of it. As we become more mindful of ourselves and our behaviors and patterns, it is evident that beneath our stories of self – who we think we are – this energy IS the foundation of our unique vibration and what we contribute to the world.

When in connection with the energetics of JOY and truth, you begin to dance and flow with Oneness – JOY in the moment, non-separation from all that surrounds you, and the ability to move through space and with less restriction and fear. The result? Seeing freedom and the beautiful choices that are all around you.

We Are Energy in Physical Form

Here are six practices I encourage you to explore:

1. Take ten minutes daily to nurture yourself with quiet love and a focused, calm breath.
2. Make hydration, healthy food, and healthy gut microbiota priorities. Research food energy and water alkalinity and purification. There is electrical energy in the food and water that penetrates our cells and skin.
3. Have healthy relationships – with yourself, others, food, and nature. Unhealthy connections are energy zappers.
4. Clear emotions (fear, anger, guilt, worry) that limit you. Get "clean" on the inside. Investigate forgiveness techniques and mantras, and learn about chakras along with the meridian system.

5. Move the body daily. Move with the intention of mindfulness and purpose, for fun rather than for an accomplishment or goal.
6. By frequently checking in with your ego and living a purpose-driven life, I know you'll feel more in tune with your inner self and enjoy the uniqueness of each moment.

Tamee's empathic and insightful ability to merge with the Divine helps her discover the unique qualities of energy within and as ONE. Her clients benefit by finding balance in mind, body, and spirit through self-exploration on many levels such as food, breath, movement, and sound. She practices and teaches Cre8tive Courageous Consciousness (C3) using one's inner dialogue to explore balance and self-expansion and find one's unique, creative source. For more information please visit her website at www.Shekhinahpath.com.

Off the Beaten Path

Jessica Louise Li

YOU KNOW HOW THEY SAY WHEN you're about to die your life flashes before your eyes? I had that chance… at the hand of my husband almost ten years into our marriage. Knowing that someone wants to maim or kill you is something that no human should experience. Nor is being at the mercy of another, begging for your life.

I left my parents' home shortly after turning seventeen, transfixed on creating a more exciting life than the boring one I thought I had lived to that point. I grew up in Edmonton, Alberta, Canada, in the '80s, in a place where people were predominantly white. In fact, I could count on both hands how many Asians were in the entire seven grades that comprised my elementary school. I was laughed at for the food I ate and teased for my "Chinky" eyes. That was the start of feeling alone, like an outsider from another country.

After years of being barraged by racist slurs, I wanted someone to save me from being Chinese. On top of that, other students would taunt me for being shy, the "girl who never talks" and who's "a crybaby." By the time I was in seventh grade, the shift started. Asian gang members who roamed the city with their yellow-streaked hair and loud, souped-up sports cars started to catch my attention. When I was in tenth grade I met twin Asian sisters at school who, despite their own nerd characteristics, were intrigued by bad boys, and talked about them in a way that brought mystery and an attractive forbiddance to these guys' dangerous lifestyle.

Edmonton had been going through a gang problem for several years, and I was there during the height of it. I was hooked by the thrill of these bad-ass boys. They were guys the public feared because they had no concern for others. Ruthless guys. I liked them. I felt like hanging around them made me a bad girl, a persona I was thrilled to embody after years of being made fun of for being a good one. I was done with quiet and shy. I wanted to show people how cool I was. I felt the tables had finally turned when I bumped into some former elementary classmates who now were the geeks, or at least "just average," and was identified as running with the gang. And I wanted to ride that wave some more.

Within the first day after moving out of my home, I met my future husband, Shawn, at an apartment that some gangsters lived in. I knew that whoever was living in that place was most likely a thug, or was at least aware of the illegal shit that went on. There, I acknowledged it; I knew what my husband was up to when I met him, even if I didn't know everything he was involved in.

Our first meeting went something like this: I walked into the apartment and he was sitting on the floor watching TV with his back against a wall. I said, "Hey," and he replied with the same greeting. Within about ten minutes I was in the bedroom having sex with one of the guys, and two minutes after he was done with me, Shawn walked in to do the same. After we finished we talked for about a minute and then he walked out of the room.

Later that day he and another gang boss told me they were going somewhere and I was to go with them. After driving down several back and side roads, we ended up at a property where drug packages were assembled and stored… and that's what we did. They taught me the ropes to get the job done, and as we were wrapping up for the evening Shawn went outside to start the car and motioned for me to join him. I climbed into the backseat as he quickly joked, "I'm going to kidnap you." He took me back to his apartment, and after more sex we fell asleep.

I woke up the next morning panicking because I had to get to class (I was anal about being on time). He tried to hold me back by taking the only money I had on me, a crisp fifty dollar bill that my mom had given me. When he took it, it felt like he'd taken a thousand dollars from my wallet. It really hurt. He told me to go to the convenience store across the street and grab a newspaper and some coffee for him. Although I can't recall the exact sentence I said to him in reply, he took it as my having an attitude, abruptly grabbed the back of my neck with his hand, and violently pushed my head towards the wall, stopping short just before hitting it. That was the first of five times he laid his hands on me.

Despite the violence, we decided to get married in August of 2000 at the jail where he was serving out a sentence for being part of a criminal organization.

Over the next few years of marriage he continued to be highly verbally abusive to me, and on three more occasions he struck me. He threatened to kill me; hit me with a toilet brush while I was pregnant with our second child, a son; threw a book at my face that left me with a black eye for a couple of weeks; smashed my makeup containers; threw ceramic cutlery at me; and violently yanked my hair.

Then came attack number five – the last straw. I was working as a personal support worker taking care of Laura, a lovely, elderly rich woman with dementia, in the Toronto area. Some weeks I worked up to eighty hours and would spend a couple of nights at her place. Let me say that being away from a husband who was controlling and jealous, even though the money was excellent, was asking for trouble.

One night, while on a sleepover shift, Shawn texted me saying one of our daughters (by that time we had three children) was bleeding. I didn't believe he'd hurt the kids, but it was enough to make me drop everything I was doing and break the speed limit driving the half-hour drive to our home. He opened the door and had that look in his eyes

115

that I knew meant bad news. I also spotted an empty bottle of liquor behind him on the living room table, which was even worse because he wasn't normally a drinker.

He wanted to talk about our relationship, and promised he wouldn't get mad. "Let's just lay it all out," he said calmly. In a matter of minutes he had punched me in the face, breaking my glasses in half. He pushed me to the sofa, got on top of me, and started to choke me with his large hands, confidently telling me, "I'll kill you. I kill people like you." I passed out. In a few minutes I regained consciousness only to have him start choking me for a second time. One of (what I thought were) my last thoughts was "This isn't fair. I didn't get to do everything I wanted to do." He finally let go of me. That very moment became my catalyst.

As I managed to stand up, I saw him slowly walk around the foyer pole and ever-so-calmly pick up a nine-inch stainless steel kitchen knife from the ledge. He walked up and stood directly in front of me. He was six feet tall and about 270 pounds, while I was five-foot-four and 130 pounds. All I could do was squeeze my eyes shut and wait for the blade to pierce the top of my head. I felt it quickly go in and out of my scalp, just enough to make me feel it. Then there was more. My heart raced and I saw death coming. It was the most afraid I'd ever been in my life. "This stuff only happens in movies," is what I tried to wrap my head around. Then he stopped. He backed off and told me I could leave the house, but I was not going to do that with my three children asleep upstairs. I was ready to face whatever he was planning if I stayed.

He threw me a towel telling me to "clean up." When my adrenaline started to wear off I started to tremble from the shock and pain. I checked in the mirror on the closet door in the foyer to see the damage as I walked by. My face was covered in purple and red dots, and was swollen. My neck had scratch marks all over it; I could still see them under the blood I'd inadvertently smeared on my face when checking for head wounds. A couple of my teeth were chipped and chunks of my

116

hair were missing. The skin on part of my right hand near my wrist was hanging and bleeding non-stop from a stab wound. He later told me that the reason he stopped stabbing me was because the rosary he was wearing during the attack broke. It snapped him out of his rage. I keep that broken piece with me as a reminder that I was being protected by angels that night.

I went to the police three months after the attack, pressed charges against him, and he was arrested. I had planned to recant my statement, but decided to follow through with the charges. I needed to think about what I wanted in life, what made me happy. As a result we physically separated in August of 2010.

I decided to start my own business, one with the purpose of helping others who had gone through similar experiences. It's amazing that I now get to help men become better partners, sons, brothers, fathers, friends, and colleagues. It's also amazing that as a holistic health coach I get to support women in their own journeys. And I founded a non-profit organization that provides a place for creative-expression healing for adults currently in abusive relationships.

I am often asked how I got through it all. I've learned that you can strip me of everything material, but one thing you can't take away is my mind and unwavering spirit. It's what allows me to plow forward even though I might not know exactly where I'm going. This second shot at life is a powerful gift I've been given. People tell me all the time, "I'm sorry to hear about what happened to you." Please don't be. I wouldn't be this strong, independent woman with a great head on her shoulders, beaming with positivity, if I hadn't been delivered from all that shit I received.

Shawn died suddenly in May of 2014. It was a shock, but I'm glad I had the opportunity to express my forgiveness, and that he had the opportunity to start rebuilding his relationships with our children.

I came to better understand the meaning of the saying "Life is short." I have three beautiful gifts called my children that I simply need to look at to be reminded of my strength and that I MUST move forward. There are no ifs, ands, or buts. Failure is not a choice in my world. That old street lifestyle is done with, and now I'm living a life of higher consciousness, happiness, and freedom.

Always remember: YOU'VE GOT YOU! Let no one take away your unwavering spirit. You're all that you have, and in this big, scary world the ONLY person responsible for moving forward is YOU.

Give gratitude, acknowledge your blessings, and appreciate those around you. Live, laugh, love, and dance. Constantly up-level yourself. You've got this. I'm living my life on my own terms now, my own "beaten path," after being on his for too long.

Jessica Louise Li helps entrepreneurs and high-achieving professionals reach new levels of wealth through the power of sexual energy. She focuses on mind-body principles and combines Eastern and Western philosophies. Jessica is the author of *High Powered Food and Fitness for the Busy Professional Woman* and of the forthcoming book, *Soul Fortified*. For details on her live events and online programs, visit www.JessicaLouiseLi.com and www. TheSensationalSexSeminar.com.

Ditching the Confines of Fear and Grief; Embracing the Freedom of Faith

Veronica Lynch, PhD

THE UNTIMELY DEATH OF MY MOTHER and the disintegration of our family when I was twelve profoundly impacted my sense of self. I felt alone, abandoned, and "less than" my peers, with an emptiness that lasted for years. Because the emptiness left me feeling broken, disconnected, and afraid, I hoped I could find a way to feel whole again.

As the eleventh of twelve children, I needed the security of my family and fondly remembered a time when we functioned more as a collective unit. We had not experienced such a profound loss before as a close-knit family, but we had experienced some losses. When I was five years old, our family dogs, Tarzan and Warrick, died. My brother and I buried them by the sea, and we did not get another dog, nor did we talk about it again. My family did not communicate openly about such things.

A couple of years later my mother went to live on another island in search of a better life, and her absence created additional feelings of loss. Two years after that she sent for my younger brother and me, the two youngest, to come and live with her. This uprooting created more feelings of loss, yet I was excited about being with my mother.

I didn't adjust quickly to my new school environment. By the time I began to feel comfortable enough to make new friends, my mother had become ill. I noticed she was not eating nor sleeping well. I began to worry about her because she grew weary very quickly. A year later, in September, my mother, looking even more tired and worn, announced that the three of us would be returning home. I continued to worry about her health and wondered what would happen to us. I was disappointed by the news of returning home, but I knew I would see my old friends again. We returned to our original home in December. Unfortunately, two months after our return, my mother passed from hardening of the arteries. Since her death was related to her diet and lifestyle, I was always curious about how to use food to prevent diet-related illnesses that lead to early death. So when the opportunity presented itself, I entered the Institute for Integrative Nutrition as a way to deepen my knowledge about nutrition.

Because the death of the matriarch affects the entire family, my relationships with my siblings were greatly impacted. We did not discuss our feelings about Mom's death or what it meant to us personally or collectively. Consequently, I did not know I had a choice in how to deal with grief, and never considered that what I thought or felt mattered, since I came from a family where children are seen and not heard. We did not know as a family how to cope with the myriad of emotions that accompanied such a loss, and there were no instructions about how to cope with bereavement.

I did not know how to talk about the multitude of emotions I was feeling as a twelve-year-old child. I did not know what to do with the feelings inside me. I thought they had to be kept secret because no one talked or communicated with me about them. I kept them all inside.

The death of my mother and not grieving collectively with my family impacted me in many ways, but especially in regard to trust.

I found it hard to trust others, including friends, family, church, myself, and God as I knew Him. Fear and lack of trust brought about loneliness, anger, shame, guilt, isolation, resentment, and insecurity. Fear kept me silent!

By not knowing how to grieve, I bought into the messages, spoken or otherwise, about how to handle my loss. I learned to grieve alone and not trust others or even share my feelings. I regretted, resented, and felt ashamed that I had lost so much in the past.

I spent the next seven years worrying about what was going to happen to me. There were times when I felt angry at my mother for leaving me and not caring about what would become of me. Because I believed she abandoned me, I abandoned myself, my siblings, and my family.

Over the years I developed a plethora of defense mechanisms to cope with multiple losses in my life. These defensive emotions became so dense that it made me wonder if grief were ever complete. I felt very angry at God, the world, and myself, and I ultimately closed off my heart and trusted no one. The crippling effects of fear and lack of trust led me to reacquaint myself with knowing that I had spiritual support, if I would just call upon it to work for my greater good.

After high school graduation I began the journey to search for peace and stability in my life. I wanted to be happy and practice the steps of exercising faith. I sought out workshops and retreats about handling grief. I took the steps needed to give me comfort, peace, acceptance, and recovery from the pain of the losses.

In 1991, I was invited to attend a dream-weaver's retreat in Colorado where I discovered journaling. Writing about what I was feeling was a helpful tool. On the last day of the retreat, I confronted God and told Him everything I could remember that had happened to me. I told Him how afraid, grief-stricken, unhappy, and sad I had been. I told Him how angry I felt at Him for allowing so many sad things to happen to me. After I had wept and purged every angry emotion

I felt, I listened for His response and heard nothing. I later came to acknowledge and accept that God had always been there; He had never left me. I could not have made it had He abandoned me.

At the dream-weaver's retreat, I learned to let go and not be too attached to anything, as life is fluid and must be free. I also came to understand and accept my share of the responsibility for feeling incomplete.

After many years of continued estrangement from my family, I was shocked to experience emotions familiar to me from my mother's passing when I got the news in 2014 that my ninety-six-year-old uncle, my mother's last living sibling, had died. The emotions that I thought had been healed were still there. I realized that something else needed to be done. I had to surrender to transformation by removing my ego. It had kept me holding on to the continued separation, anger, and lack of trust. I was then ready to open myself up to the collective grieving of my family.

I understand now that the whole family had probably been grieving the loss of our matriarch all these years and we had not allowed ourselves to grieve openly as a family.

Courage Stands in Faith

Despite the many doubts and setbacks, I never thought of giving up. There was always something deep inside ushering me to believe that I could find peace, trust, and joy in my life. That something I chose to call faith. Faith is the opposite of fear. Faith eradicates fear. When fear is gone, light appears. Love appears.

What I have learned is that you have to be open to love in whatever form it shows up. We are truly here to love and help one another. I believe that the most important asset we have is our relationships with those we love.

Whole Family Grief

For all that I had been through, it was hard for me to become aware of the fact that I had not completely recovered from grieving. From my uncle's death, I gained awareness about what was incomplete in my emotional relationship with my family nucleus.

Families should be encouraged to grieve collectively so that they can complete any unfinished business. Quite often, especially in large families, focus is placed on the individual grief process and not on the family recovering together. Sharing and exchanging support from family members at a time of grief seems vital for recovery.

Coping Then and Now – What I've Learned

After reading *The Grief Recovery Handbook* by John W. James and Frank Cherry, I completed a graph of my loss history, a relationship graph of my grief, and discovered some undelivered communication. I became aware of the many losses that had occurred in my life, so many of which had gone unnoticed or had been buried. I learned that you don't have to grieve alone.

The transition of my uncle made me aware of how faith had been operating in my life even during the times when I wasn't paying attention. I had not let my family into my life or heart all that time; hence I was still harboring feelings of abandonment, mistrust, and secrecy. Recognizing this, I surrendered to take the journey through faith to open my heart, reunite with my family, and grieve collectively so that we all could be free.

My transformation took place when I chose to change my mindset about the family secrets, and past regrets, and to open my heart and let my family and siblings in so we could reconnect. I shared grief recovery resources with my family. It's been over forty years and we are now organizing our first ever family reunion next year.

Healing artist, **Veronica R. Lynch, PhD,** has twenty years of experience as a licensed clinical social worker and psychotherapist to adolescents, children, and families, promoting better health and mental wellness. As creator of the *7 Balancing Acts to Wholeness: A Path to Revitalization,* she helps people raise their life-force energy to put an end to suffering and replace it with a new and vital life. Dr. Veronica can be reached at www.CreateWhole.com.

Championing Life and Love – The Secrets to an Inspired Destiny!

Sarah Jane Michaels

I am strong, because I have known great weakness.
I am fearless, because I have faced my worst illusions.
I am beautiful, because pain has not dimmed my inner light.
I am loving, because I have lost all and yet I heartily love again.
I am wise, because I have listened to the whispers of higher wisdom.
I am joyous, because my champion spirit weaves wonders in my destiny!

CAN YOU RECALL A TIME IN YOUR LIFE when you sensed you were on the brink of monumental change? You were about to experience an electric redirection in your life's journey. Change was beating a rhythm in your heart that would not stop — it only grew louder with a powerful momentum.

Perhaps you realized you needed a victorious spirit to transit your circumstances, for the day had come when the risk of remaining in a tight bud was more painful than the risk of blooming toward a desired goal. In that moment you were compelled to create a future that never existed before – even though everything you hoped for was vulnerable in the wilds of change.

In the course of life, my own massive transitions have required me to brave the battering of multiple storms before the longed-for dreams burst through like a new dawn. One particular tumultuous and transformational year in my life forged a striking pathway to a *brand new* reality being born.

As you read on, you'll discover how my destiny path weathered wild gales of bleak destruction. The pain endured on the way was enormous. It was only at the last hurdle that I withered like a battered flower stem. In fact, by the end of that year, the old me had been annihilated. I couldn't recognize my own life! Ultimately though, it all led to the beauty of miracles and scintillating love.

The Prelude – A Destiny Set-Up!

I once read that the future enters into us, in order to transform itself within us, long before it happens. I have found this to be impressively true. You see I was only eleven when I spoke to an audience of hundreds on the topic of "Love Is…" Winning the highest speaking award that night, I was acclaimed an "Angel of Love."

In truth, I knew in my entire being that illustrious night that one day I could be a global messenger of love. Today I am an international bestselling author, speaker, and relationships expert, with one of my latest books, *Love: It's Like Glitter for Your Soul,* making waves around the world.

There is no doubt that walking the path of a purposeful life offers transformation at many perilous precipice points. One of my most dramatic challenges swung into motion on a gloriously sunny morning that revealed no hint of the dark abyss gaping in front of me. At the time I was thirty-eight years of age.

That morning, as I communicated with the Divine in meditation, I humbly pledged my service to uplifting humanity and inspiring audiences on an even broader worldwide scale. *"God. Do as You will with my body, my mind, and my life, so that I may offer the highest work possible as a vehicle for LOVE."*

I believe that life is like a steering wheel; it only takes one bold move to change your entire direction, but I absolutely did NOT expect what happened next.

A Curve Ball the Size of a Giant Asteroid!

It is extraordinary that three days later my body and mind were ravaged by a sudden stroke! I collapsed to the floor, my ten-month-old baby beside me as I fell into a dysfunctional pile of body and limbs. My life had changed in an instant, and that instant would guarantee *total* life transformation.

The pain of a stroke can be over in a flash. Everything that comes after is the pain of realization and the pain of recovery. In the minutes that followed my collapse into helplessness, I knew my brain was wounded. Yet Rumi's teachings would never be far from me – "The wound is the place where Light enters you."

The most incredible thing happened spontaneously as I experienced near death. I suddenly accelerated at enormous speed into the all-encompassing love of the Pure Divine/God. No longer was I an individual consciousness. I was ONE with ALL in a vast field of DIVINITY. I was HOME. I was LOVE. I was CREATION itself.

Reawakening from Tragedy into an Evolutionary Shift

I awoke miraculously a day later to the experience of my soul trying to merge with a damaged body. I was unable to speak, walk, read, or write properly, and it was shocking that I had no memory of my physical body's life prior to the stroke. I did not even know the names of my four young children!

Can you understand being catapulted into a whole new life experience – or at least shoved up so hard against the face of disability that it forces you to rethink your idea of who you are and how your body works? Ultimately, though, like everything in life, it is not what happens to you, but how you insightfully respond to it that counts.

As the mounting tragedies of dysfunction dawned on me, I realized that there were two ways in which I could respond to my debilitating circumstances: I could 1) react with utter dismay at the intellectual and physical impairment, or 2) seek liberation from the suffering via a creative force and make myself stronger, better than before.

I chose the latter. After all, Zen teachings say that once you open up to the inevitability of your demise, you can begin to transform that situation. This was my evolutionary moment – a climactic vehicle for *re-creation* via physical transformation in partnership with the Divine.

The Power of Transformation and Miracles

When working with the power of creation, real life can appear stranger than science fiction. I grew an unbelievable one and a half inches overnight (3.8 cm.), lost fifteen and a half pounds in seven days (7 kg.), reconstructed the neural pathways in my brain, and substantially changed the visual appearance of my hands and face. The thrust of continuous faith was the firewood that fueled my miraculous transformation.

It is remarkable that I gained a full physical recovery from the stroke in only seven months. To say that my doctors were baffled would be an understatement. They declared me a "medical mystery."

The Pain of Great Loss –
Into an Annihilation Zone!

The Universe was quite astoundingly not done with me yet! My transformational year was soon to dive into the darkest of pits before the light shone brilliantly. Next I discovered that hearts are utterly breakable!

Toward the final stages of my recovery from the debilitating stroke, my husband of seventeen years unexpectedly abandoned our family, leading to a crisis of epic proportions. With brutal harshness he spoke these unforgettable words: "I don't love you anymore. I don't want a wife and four kids. I want a bachelor lifestyle. And I don't care if you and the kids are out on the streets!"

Grievous loss finally closed in on me. The stroke didn't break me, but my husband's multiple affairs and acrid betrayal did. Via life-altering circumstances I lost the man I had loved for two decades, my million-dollar home, my business, and my lifestyle through his vicious separation agenda.

What's more, as a single mother there were despairing times when I couldn't even feed my hungry children. My spirit was squashed into a blackened, bleak hole of existence.

As you, too, probably know, emotional pain is a pesky part of being human. A gouging wound to the heart is a hurt that can't be ignored. Yet the most authentic qualities about human existence are our capacities to overcome, to endure, to transform, to create, to love fully once again, and to be greater than our past pains.

The Breakthrough to a New Way of Loving and Connecting

Still bearing the wounds of a broken heart, I eventually chose not to listen to the inner cries of shattered dreams and mountainous suffering. Instead I listened to the voices of higher wisdom.

Every night as I lay in the vastness of my king-sized bed, I was not really alone. I was wrapped in the gloriously loving arms of angels while my tears were gently wiped away. *"Search for your inner light; it will guide you,"* the angelic beings encouraged. *"Choose to feel an inner peace; it will nourish you. Embrace the voice of inner love; it will heal you. Let this journey transform you; and it will bring you toward a Divine Love."*

During this breakthrough time, I was being called to "walk my talk" of mastery as an educator in love, relationships, parenting, and sexuality. I knew that pure love was a force more formidable than any other. This energy of love, while invisible, was powerful enough to transform me inside and out. Love would not be vanquished from my soul or life!

The Joys of Scintillating Love

For twelve weeks I worked on myself diligently, every daylight hour, communing with Divine guidance to heal the savage hurts of the past. Virtually no inner wound was left unhealed. I knew that analysis alone would not transform me. I still needed to do the changing myself. Therefore my wounds would catapult me into the best and most beautiful reinvention of myself.

Every seed of doubt that sprung to life was diligently cleared from my consciousness. In their place I seeded love, joy, gratitude, and self-belief.

In all honesty, at one point during these evolutionary months, uncertainty briefly infiltrated my mind to conjure dismaying images of an unfulfilled romantic future. The risk of being hungry for a loving partnership with a soulmate seemed all too real. *"Who would want to marry a woman with four kids?"* my desolate thoughts groaned.

However, my feminine spirit would not tolerate the putrid dullness of imagined lack of love. So day after day I powerfully drew upon my metaphysical and spiritual knowledge to call in my "twin-flame" partner, knowing that with this Divine union a profound relationship could be built on all levels.

I do believe the Universe is full of magical things. Heavenly love can be experienced on earth, especially through placing a "cosmic order" and doing the inner work. In my case, a soulful partnership quickly came into sensational manifestation. Through the glow of true love's kisses the remnants of my grief were turned to beauty. "Soul love" completely reinvented my life, and two more precious babies were born from my womb. Each day now contains an exquisiteness of love that is wondrous, spiritual, stimulating, challenging, and enriching.

Orchestrating Greatness

So how did I achieve such miraculous results in my life? Well, I'll let you in on a little secret. People who are able to remain lovingly focused in pursuit of their most valued aspirations are the ones who are highly likely to become champions in their quests. I chose to be a champion in my own life, and you can, too.

Plus, I think you'll agree that when you partner with the Divine it's like getting on a supersonic train intent on a masterful destination, although sometimes the speed can appear out of your control! Occasionally you may feel unbalanced, or even distressed, by the unexpected twists and turns.

Let's face it; monumental change or the quest for love is a process — sometimes the illusions of setbacks occur. Yet when things feel as if they are falling apart, they may actually be falling into place. Somehow the Universe always finds a way to orchestrate greatness, where the human life you were fashioning gives way to the soulful life you are destined to live.

Finally, as you journey on your unique path of life and love, I encourage you to consider these insightful words by Socrates: "The secret of change is to focus all of your energy, not on fighting the old, but on building the new."

International relationships expert and multiple bestselling author, **Sarah Jane Michaels,** aka The Love Magnet, increases people's chances of striking a true love match. Through her highly successful strategies, programs, and live events, she offers the essential ingredients for relationship transformation, love re-ignition, and even beautiful breakups. If you need help with your love life, get started with your FREE *Finding True Love* video series, or for relationship fulfillment claim your FREE *Marriage Saver* product at www.SarahJaneMichaels.com.

cᘛ

One Heck of a Day

Gina Morse, MS, Ed. Counseling

PROVERBIAL BAD DAYS... WE ALL HAVE THEM. Some are worse than others. Some people have more of them than others. Have you ever questioned their meaning, the purpose, the why? Do you chalk them up to bad luck? Do you take the perspective that you must have done something terribly wrong and that you're being punished for sitting in judgment of yourself, tearing yourself apart remembering every mistake you believe you've made to verify your reasoning, setting your good old cognitive dissonance in full motion to make your perspective true?

Do you blame and shame yourself endlessly? Or do you go in the opposite direction and blame someone else or circumstances that were beyond your control, stepping into a victim mentality? You start remembering every detail of times past when so-and-so did this or that to you, or this or that happened, and ask, "Why me? Why again?"

I used to do all of the above and then some. But what if there is a profound explanation? What if there is a deeper truth, a reason beyond that, which you haven't explored – a real truth, a Divine intervention created and designed for your good and the good of all?

Valentine's Day 2014

By human definition, February 14th, 2014, was a disaster. I recall the order of the day's events perfectly: I lost my fantastic job. I was told the devastating news at a doctor's appointment that my organs could start shutting down any minute and was advised to take six months off from work – being a single mother of two daughters, that wasn't an option. My boyfriend broke up with me after eight years in the most inhuman way possible. My water heater broke down and flooded my basement, leaving me with no hot water. My car battery died, and on my way to fix it a stone kicked up by an eighteen-wheeler that passed me on the highway cracked my windshield.

It was as if a tsunami had struck my world. Just one of those events would constitute a bad day. I've had more than my fair share of bad days, but all this in one day? Really? It didn't feel real even though I knew it was. I felt broken. The humanness part of me felt shattered beyond repair, like a fragile glass ornament that had dropped on the floor; nothing left but a million pieces with no hope of repair. It felt like my life was gone. I had woken up with one life and went to bed with another, one I didn't recognize.

Fast Flashback

I used to be known as the "professional overcomer," and that title came to be through bouncing back from a variety of extremely challenging adversities: a severely emotionally abusive ten-year marriage and exceptionally difficult divorce; two other previous job losses; raising two daughters alone; a history of emotionally abusive relationships; rape; two identity thefts; and several other obstacles stemming from various broken systems in our world today. The very worst was the day that I almost lost my fifteen-year-old daughter due to complications from a blood disorder after a tonsillectomy. That one

134

was by far the most transformational for me, but my overall score earned me the title.

Each and every struggle brings about learning and a personal transformation. Each one also allows me to help those I work with more effectively. There is much truth in the saying "God never gives you more than you can handle." Everything is okay, even when you think it's not; even when it feels terrible. It's all been Divinely orchestrated for your good and the good of all.

Challenges

When you step into challenging issues and trying times, as difficult as it may seem, DO NOT PANIC! Be still. Get quiet. Breathe. Remember that there is a difference between having faith and living it. Just saying you have faith isn't enough. Living faith is actually being in the action of faith – being able to truly stay in peace even through difficult times and really trust that all will be okay; because truly it will be. It is being able to stay out of fear and at the same time accept it, love it, and step fully into it, knowing that you are truly, fully loved and supported by the Divine. He has you and won't let you fall even though you feel like you will. Don't worry – He won't let you. Living faith is being able to be in peace even in the midst of a storm. It is truly being able to give it over to the Divine and really know that all will be as it should.

I was in shock from the trauma of all that loss all in the same day. Stay out of your mind; it lies to you! Your mind makes up stories about what happened that aren't true and that cause you to unnecessarily suffer more. It tells you bad things will happen that won't, and that good things won't happen that will.

Take your own fast flashback. Draw strength from the worst thing you think you have ever been through. Take note that you are still here and find peace in that. It's even better if you can identify what you learned and the gifts you received from that "worst thing." After I almost lost my daughter I made a plaque of one my favorite quotes that reads, "What if you woke up today with only what you thanked God for yesterday?" I have started every day since that almost fateful day with that question. It's a game-changing opening to each day. It brings me instant peace and puts things into perspective.

We can't take the human out of a human, and even with as much practice as I've had over the years with the challenging circumstances I've faced, I still felt alone, overwhelmed, and crushed when I was hit with a lot of loss all at once that day. But God never takes away what He doesn't replace, and He always replaces it with something better.

I was also curious and excited, because clearly I had been cleaned out. God's timing is perfect timing, so practice patience. Everyone knows me as a super positive person, keeping others uplifted and smiling. That person had to go on vacation, but I knew I wanted her back as soon as possible. What we resist persists. I had to step into acceptance of those losses and pain with appreciation, view them for what they really were – open doors, and make room for blessings to get to the other side.

Things don't happen to you, but through you, so another helpful hint is to not take them personally. It was necessary for me to check out and check up; connect to the only connection that counts. For forty-one days I just spent time with God. I unplugged from the world. I prayed, read scripture, and meditated. I wanted to know why all this had shown up in my life. I wanted answers. Ask and you shall receive.

My Job Loss

I have known for at least the last five years that my purpose here is to help people with transformational breakthroughs in their lives. So it shouldn't have been a shock when tension in the system at work heated up over the last year I was there. I can even remember times when a voice deep within me said that even though I was good at what I was doing, I should be contributing and playing in a bigger way. But

I didn't pay attention to my tension. It was easier to stay comfortable with what I knew, what I liked, and what was financially stable.

Though it has been a stretching experience, I'm currently working on my life's purpose and trusting God to unfold it in His perfect time. I'm staying in alignment with my values and my authentic self and giving the rest up. God is giving me permission to do what I love! If I hadn't lost my job, you wouldn't be reading this chapter right now, so He is unfolding opportunities and opening doors. I'm paying attention.

My Health Struggles

A holistic practitioner showed up in my life who allowed me to pay him what my treatments would have cost if I'd had health insurance. After my flexible spending account ran out, his wife traded the cost of treatments for my coaching services – God opening those doors again. Watch for the blessings!

Like people who diet and fall off the wagon, I struggle with putting and keeping weight on. Life patterns are hard to break. The warnings that showed up for me were blessings reminding me to keep a close watch for those patterns, as they can sneak up on me if I stop paying attention. I'm currently forcing myself to get on the scales daily to track that potentially harmful pattern and keep it in check.

My Love Loss

The question becomes "What loss?" Did I really want a future with a man who didn't really love, respect, and value me? Of course not! In reflection I could see how I had convinced myself that the relationship was healthy, but of course it wasn't. I wasn't listening to my God-given intuition, my "God guts." But God knew and He stepped in. He was protecting me, just like He has with my health.

After that relationship ordeal was finally behind me, another relationship was the last thing on my mind, and I thought that was the last thing God would address on the list of my pressing concerns. However, God works on His own agenda, not mine, and I let him. Even though it was totally unexpected, the most amazing guy on the planet showed up for me. God not only protected me, God promoted me! This new man respects me, values me, and appreciates me for my authentic, real-deal self. I was never after a perfect guy, just the perfect guy for me, and he is. I have the healthy relationship I've always asked God for, my forever love, my happily-ever-after.

Gifts

Are bad days really bad days? What if bad days are really great days? What if, in truth, your worst days are your brightest blessings? How would viewing a bad day from that perspective change how you address one? The more difficult the day, the grander and greater the gifts. That Valentine's Day was my wake-up call for paying closer attention to old patterns slipping back in, and more consistently connecting. I'm now dropping in hourly!

We don't like to wake up with ice water thrown in our faces, but if you aren't getting up and someone who loves you does that to save you from missing the most exciting opportunity in your life, would you consider it a blessing? Sometimes you have to be shaken up pretty good. God awakens you by whatever means necessary, even if at times with the proverbial 2x4, but only out of love and because He cares and wants to protect you. He wants to give you permission to have the things you want in life; to live, stretch, and grow; and to express yourself at the highest level of your most authentic self. He clears the path of obstacles that prevent you from achieving your highest potential. When he sends you a wake-up call, he is allowing for promotions, opportunities, open doors, and possibilities that would not otherwise be available to you. He is clearing you out of your own way. He is redirecting you, guiding you, leading you, and teaching you like the loving Father He is. He is protecting you from harm's way, from individuals, from circumstances, and sometimes even from yourself. Don't fight Him as a child fights with their parents. Just as we can see what our children can't, God sees what we can't. Everything is 100 percent created and designed for your good and the good of all – to thrive, not just survive. Everything happens for a reason, and they're all for good.

Gina Morse, MS, Ed. Counseling, is known as the Spiritual Transformational Expert, as well as an author, inspirational speaker, and energetic and uplifting coach. Helping women emerge triumphant from tragedy, discover their true authentic selves, and recognize their value and worth is Gina's passion. If you are struggling with adversity, visit www.GinaMorseTransformations.com to receive a free session, her daily affirmation, tips, and news on the release of her forthcoming book, *Shift Shockers*.

It's Not about You

Neale Donald Walsch

I'VE LEARNED THAT MY WORK IN THE WORLD is not about me at any level: it's about the message that was offered to me to send to the world. My story, in brief, is really quite simple.

I had reached the lowest point of my life, where nothing was working. My relationship with my significant other had fallen apart, my livelihood had utterly and completely disappeared, my health was rapidly going downhill, and then, to make matters worse, I had an automobile accident in which I broke my neck.

I realized at that juncture that I did not want to live my life anymore in the way I had been living it. I knew that something important had to change. I just didn't know what it was, specifically, nor did I know how to do it, and I became more and more frustrated as my life went further and further downhill.

After I had my accident, I wound up living on the streets because I ran out of government social benefits. I dropped through the safety net that our society puts up for people who are in trouble. And, finally, I wound up with no money at all, thinking, "Well, this is just a temporary setback. This will just be for a week or two – a couple of months at best – and I'll get myself back on my feet." But I never got to that place in that period of time. It took me a year to get myself back together. And that year that I spent on the street was one of the most extraordinary and important periods of my life.

The most extraordinary event of my life, however, occurred *after* I got *off* the streets. I finally found a part-time job. Part of the problem was that I couldn't work at a normal job because I had a broken neck. I was walking around with a Philadelphia collar, a therapeutic device, and no one would hire me because they saw that I was obviously having severe health problems and they did not want any insurance claims filed by me once I started working with their company. All they could see was a person who was broken and was unable to do much heavy lifting or hard work. I could push a pencil, but that was about it, and there weren't any pencil pushing jobs available at that time. So I was largely just unemployable.

Then I finally got a little part-time weekend job at a local radio station as an on-air personality, and I thought, "Well, okay. Fair enough. I'm now off and running back into the world of work." Sure enough, that part-time job turned into a full-time job at the radio station about four months later, and I thought, "Okay. Life is going to work out."

That's when I really hit the skids, psychologically speaking, because after getting back into the swing of things I was confronted with the utter emptiness of my life. There I was again, working full time, in some cases ten, twelve, and even fourteen hours a day, coming home exhausted. I was just making enough money to pay my bills and keep a roof over my head while putting some food in the table, but not much else. And I thought to myself, "Wait a minute. Is this really all there is? Is it just about day-to-day, week-to-week, month-to-month survival? Is that all there is to life? And the one with the most toys in the end wins?" Because if that's all there was, then I didn't want to play anymore. If life had no greater meaning than that and no greater purpose, no greater goal or objective, I just don't want to do this anymore.

I was fifty years old and had been on this planet a half century and I couldn't find any larger reason or purpose for existing. That's when I woke up one morning at 4:15 upset with life, with God, with my whole situation, looking forward to another twenty years or more of pointless activity. And so I called out to God, "What does it take to make life work?" There I was, sitting on the couch in my living room, feeling very frustrated and at odds with the world.

Just before I fell asleep on the sofa I heard a voice. I could swear that it was right in the room with me, as it was a physical sound, a physical voice, asking me if I was ready to really hear the answers to my questions. And I awoke hearing that voice, absolutely certain there was someone in the room with me. Of course, there wasn't, at least not physically.

I looked around and the voice continued, "Would you like answers to these questions?" And I thought, "Yeah, if you've got them." At first, I thought I was just talking to myself, the way we all do once in a while. Then I came to understand very quickly that I was connecting with a much higher source, because my whole physical being was filled with radiance. I hate to sound hackneyed and so trite, but it did feel that way. I was filled with radiance, warmth, life, and light, such as to make me almost weep at the feeling of it. Tears of joy and relief streamed down my face all the while as I was sitting on my sofa at that early hour of the morning.

So I began to write my questions out. "What does it take to make life work? What's the point of all this? Somebody give me the rules. I promise I'll play. Just give me the doggone rule book! And... don't change the rules halfway through the game."

Then I received all of the information that can now be found in my books. Tons and tons and tons of questions were answered. Questions I never even thought to ask were already answered.

I wound up with many, many yellow legal pads of "dictation" at the end of this period of my life. It was my habit to jot down notes, grocery lists, those sorts of things, on yellow legal pads, so I happened to have two or three lying around the house. Those three legal pads got filled up very quickly. A couple of days later I ran to the office supply store and purchased more. Before I knew it, I had fifteen or twenty of them filled with these kinds of dialogues that were now taking place on a daily basis.

I was told that these writings would one day become a book. I thought to myself, "Of course! Yes! I can see myself now, sending these pages off to a publisher telling them that God is talking to me." But, in fact, that's just what I did. I thought, "Well, you know what? This will be interesting. It will be kind of like proof this really happened to me."

I realized, of course, that publishers get 1,500+ unsolicited manuscripts a month from everyone in the world wanting to write the next great book, and they hardly open them, much less read and evaluate them, unless they come from an agent or from someone they trust. I knew my chances were slim to none. But I sent it off anyway.

Well, I was right, it seemed at first. My book of dictation notes was rejected by four of the five publishers that I sent it to. And even the fifth publisher, the one that actually finally put it out, didn't accept it until my second sending. Their response went, "Thank you for your submission. Unfortunately, your book does not fit our titles list. We wish you well with your endeavor."

But I sent it back to that fifth publisher because I was angry. I said, "Look, you guys. You didn't even read the book. I know that because if you had read it, you could not say it did not fit your titles list, *because all you publish are metaphysical books.*"

Then I did a very daring thing. I did not send a letter with my second sending of the manuscript. All I did was tear off a page of my yellow legal pad and I scribbled on a note: "Read any ten pages!" And, you know what? The publisher took me up on the dare. Good old Bob Friedman, who has since become a good friend, picked up the book and read ten pages at random. He told me later that he immediately reached for the phone and called me.

He said, "Listen, we want to publish this book," and I was both delighted and shocked. And he did publish it. They put it on the fast track and it was published twelve to fourteen weeks after that. Three months later it landed on the *New York Times* bestseller list, where it remained for two and a half years. That book was *Conversations With God: An Uncommon Dialogue (Book 1)*.

That's when I realized that I had something here and that when God makes promises, She doesn't kid around. She means exactly what she says.

Since that time I've continued with the process. I allowed myself to be inspired, to continue that writing and dialogue for eight more books, and for a number of follow-up texts expanding on those concepts. This allowed me to explain them more fully, as I understand them, and to share them even more deeply than I could in a simple dialogue. And that's what the twenty-seven books have produced. And I continue to write, with my latest books, *The Only Thing That Matters* published in the fall of 2012, and *What God Said,* published in autumn, 2013.

I've since realized that grace was at work in my life, that something was afoot, something much higher than I, individually and personally, could ever possibly put into place. And I realized that because the book remained on the *New York Times* list for two and a half years. Ultimately, the *Conversations With God* books have reached fifteen million people in thirty-seven languages. I don't want to appear as if I'm bragging or boasting by noticing that. I'm simply indicating that's what happens when the energy is moving with a project and nothing can stop it from happening, including you.

I think that one cannot try to write a bestseller – nor can one, for that matter, try to save the planet or try to change the world. When a person fearlessly, fully, and completely enters into an expression of one's Self, of whom and what one imagines one's Self to be, then life becomes a process of expressing Oneself at the highest and grandest level that one can possibly imagine. We don't do it for the reasons of changing the world, writing a bestseller, becoming successful, or being a so-called transformational author. It's all very lovely to speak in those terms, but that isn't the ultimate purpose of it. The ultimate purpose is self-realization and self-expression, and experiencing and expressing our true identity as an aspect of the Divine. From that point, all the rest emerges automatically without an effort. Personally, I don't know how to sit down and write a bestseller, much less seven of them.

When the writing is done with none of those exterior goals in mind, then whatever happens will happen – and it will all be perfectly okay with you. Doing anything – practicing law, becoming a plumber, cleaning the floor, washing the dishes – when the "doingness" is merely an expression of the "beingness" that one has chosen to love, and when one allows that "beingness" to flow through one's self as an expression of the highest and grandest notion of who they are… that's the highest calling. When that's the reason one is writing, then, of course, the writing informs and serves to co-create the next expression of what one seeks to know one's Self as.

So if I seek to know myself as love, clarity, wisdom, understanding, patience, compassion and all the other aspects of divinity that I hold dear, that I value – if that's the reason that I'm picking up the pen or putting my fingers on the keyboard, and it's not to finish the book by Thursday or somehow make a point in this particular chapter, but rather that I am writing in a flow of consciousness – then the consciousness creates the writing and then the writing creates the consciousness. This process is circular: one thing creates another, and it has no particular aim or goal except for the circular expression of "beingness" itself.

When I came to understand the reaction that people were having around the world to *Conversations with God,* one of my biggest challenges was writing the second book, as you can imagine. Because the first book was really just a free flowing-of-consciousness dialogue that I was having with God. That free flow of conscious writing continued even after what became book one was signed to be published, but then God had told me there would be three books. So I kept writing, but it was a constant process of getting myself out of the way.

146

If I had one piece of advice for those who want to become transformational authors, it would be to get yourself out of the way. Get out of your own personal hopes, dreams, visions, ideas, income, expectations – everything, and know that the book is not about you and somehow solving your problems, elevating your lifestyle, or whatever you imagine the book is going to do for you. If you don't or can't do that, it's going to be difficult to write it in a way that it captures the human heart and expresses the mysteries of the human soul. On the other hand, if you can manage to remove yourself from the process and keep the flow moving through you from the ultimate source of wisdom in the Universe that I happen to call God, your writing will stand a much better chance of being noticed.

It took me nearly three years to complete the third book in the *Conversations With God* series. After three books in five years, I finally almost collapsed with the exertion of it. I just let go of all my expectations, including those I didn't know were there – those hidden ones under the table, the subconscious expectations.

I just said, "Okay. I'll just give all the money back. I'll just write them a check and give all the money back. I don't want to hear about the money, I don't want to hear about the fame. I don't want to hear about the so-called literary glory. I don't want to hear about the bestseller list or being on *Good Morning America* or Jay Leno. I don't want to hear about any of that. I just want to find the purity again. Help me find the purity again."

Once your path in this world has been made known to you in some way, and your being is expressing that purely in the world as you move into your role, you'll become a humanitarian – a leader if you will. Leadership is an extraordinary experience. I have been called a so-called "spiritual leader" – or one of the "leaders of the New Thought Movement." I'm not sure that's an accurate description, but I've been called that by a number of people, in the media, press, television, and so forth. So I've had to look closely at, "What is leadership?"

If you intend to be a transformational author or leader of any sort, you'll need to confront that question as well, because your work in the world may put you in what others call a place of leadership, whether you intended to be there or not. If you think that you can write a transformational book and not be thrust into a place of leadership, think again. So you need to be aware of what true leadership is, and I want to share this with you:

A leader is not one who says, "Follow me." A true leader is one who says, "I'll go first." You are going to have to demonstrate the courage, conviction, and the commitment to go first. And to go first in what? To go first in two things. First, questioning the prior assumption that you and others around you have had about everything: about money, love, God, sex, spirituality, health, everything. All the prior assumptions by which humanity lives will need to be questioned. And second, to go first in asking the great questions, "What if what I thought was so, is not so? What if I could create in my reality a different experience and a different expression of what is? What if I imagine that the whole world, every person on the planet, not just my spouse, my children, my grandchildren, my friends and neighbors, and others around me like my colleagues and associates, but every human being was watching me and using me as the model of how life could best be lived and how humanity could best be expressed? In what way, if at all, would my own behaviors change tomorrow?"

That's a huge question. The opportunity and the invitation is not to be knocked over by it, but just to live into it. If you do, your life will change overnight.

Neale Donald Walsch has written twenty-eight books on spirituality and its practical application in everyday life. His most recent books are *What God Said,* released in October 2013, and *God's Message to the World: You've Got Me All Wrong,* released in October 2014 from Rainbow Ridge Books. Neale has created several outreach projects, including the Conversations With God (CWG) Foundation, Humanity's Team, and *The Global Conversation,* an internet newspaper generating a worldwide discussion of CWG principles as they relate to daily life. All of these platforms are accessible at www.CWGPortal. com, and all are dedicated to helping the world move from violence to peace, from confusion to clarity, and from anger to love.

I AM Alive:
Living Life Liberated

Keya Murthy, BSc, MS, Clinical Hypnotherapist

Beginnings

"What I ask for, I ask in error — What I get, I do not need."
—Rabindranath Tagore

GROWING UP, I OFTEN HEARD MY MOTHER sigh and say the words above in Bengali, my mother tongue. My father is a Telegu. Interracial marriage was not socially acceptable in the 1960s in India. My siblings and I grew up rejected by our extended families and most of Indian society. Whenever there was displeasure in any form around me, I withdrew and told myself, *I do not want anything. Everything is an illusion.* Tagore's words have been my lifelong truth.

Understanding

In 1989, now living in the USA, I started working as a software engineer. In 1996 my husband and I started a software consulting firm that we co-managed besides working our full-time jobs. In 2001, with the change in the political-economic situation in the world, most of the software jobs were being outsourced to India and I lost my six-figure job. I continued working as a software consultant from home and also became an Herbalife distributor. I was overwhelmed juggling home and work. At the age of thirty-eight I found myself materially successful by most standards, yet I felt like a complete failure in my personal life. As I wanted to find the missing ingredient in my dissatisfied life, so I decided to leave my home in Dallas and travel to the Himalayas.

I went to the Tung Nath temple, which at 18,000 feet above sea level is like an island in the sky. I sat on a rock at the edge of the temple courtyard and meditated. I opened my eyes and gazed through the clouds at the village below in the valley. I wondered how every right action I'd made could yield a result so wrong. I had everything most women from India would envy: education; work experience; a husband; children; life in the USA; no financial burden of extended family, parents, and siblings; doing well in health and finances; yet nothing made sense to me in life except my three children. I felt stuck in a loveless marriage. I felt cheated and lied to, hopelessly frustrated, and ready to walk away from all my achievements and possessions if only I could find peace within me that I could keep. I was at the lowest point in my personal life, yet sitting at the highest point on the planet that one could climb to without an oxygen mask.

I asked myself and the Universe, "What's wrong with me?" There was no response. So then I asked, "What should I do now?" No answer came for that either, and walking away from my husband and children was not an option. I felt I needed to find my purpose and understand the age-old question, "Who am I?" I felt I needed to ignore the demands of Indian culture and heed my soul's cry. All I truly wanted was to detangle myself from my web of thoughts and emotions. I was willing to do whatever it took to earn this freedom.

My inner child said, "I love to sing and dance. Let's do that!" My inner critic responded, "No one will pay you to sing and dance." My mother had always said, "A woman with no money of her own is a woman with no respect of her own." I needed to know what to do so I could sustain myself while maintaining my dignity and sanity. So I asked myself what I was good at doing. The response was "I am good at being happy, healthy, fearless, and loving." I then said to myself, *I think other people want to feel happy, healthy, safe, and loved. This is how I will make a living.* I did not know what that would look like, but I trusted that the answer would come.

I still blamed by husband, my mother, my father, and the Indian culture at large for all the horrible things they had done out of their own insecurity that resulted in my feeling that my life was going nowhere. In the Bhagavad Gita (an ancient Indian text that is part of Hindu tradition), we are told that when we do what's right we'll get good results, and when we do what's wrong we'll get bad results. So I wondered how it was that when I did all the right things I still managed to get all the wrong results.

I know my mother did what was right as demanded by the society and within her means, yet she was stuck in a struggle. My mother and my father are the best mother and father I could ask for. They love me and stood up for me as good parents should. Yet they constantly argued over money and in-laws. I grew up hating money and marriage. Aha! My two breakthroughs came from this realization. No wonder I found myself in a marriage to a wonderful man yet completely lacking love! Plus the career I'd had as a software engineer for twelve years was over and I found myself penniless with no source of income.

Acceptance

My mother did the best she could with what she had and knew, yet there always seemed to be a pile of misunderstandings and misgivings between what she taught me and how I felt. I believe my mother took out all the frustrations of her own life on her husband and children

153

despite the fact that we all loved each other unconditionally. I blamed my grandparents for my mother's miseries; my resentment for my situation had now escalated to blaming my grandparents.

My mother was the second child and daughter to her parents. India, being a patriarchal society, does not fancy daughters, especially if they are born one after the other to a couple with no sons. My mother was rejected at birth and raised by her grandparents. In British India, girls in rural areas did not go to school, hence she was homeschooled. When she was ready to take her board exams, East Bengal had become East Pakistan, a Muslim nation merciless to Hindus and women in general. My mother tapped in to the tiger spirit of Bengal and moved to Calcutta to pursue her education and a free life in a secular nation. The reality was different from what she'd hoped. By this time India had gained independence from British rule and my mother found herself a refugee in her own country. I blamed the partition of India by the British for the miseries of my mother.

I wondered how my grandparents could abandon their daughter. I needed to gain more insight as to how they could have sent their child away to be raised by grandparents. I thought about the fact that my grandmother was only thirteen when she married. She arrived at the household of her in-laws as an extra pair of hands to serve. Soon she was in her mid-teens and a mother of two daughters. A child had turned into a mother without having any time to grow into a girl or be a woman. I resented the Indian culture. I realized that the fate of women in these ancient, rigid cultures came from the dormant state of spirit. I resolved to break the chain with me. I promised myself that my daughter would have a freer life than the women who came before her. I also promised myself that my boys would learn to respect women as equals.

When it came to standing up for their wives, my grandfather, my father, and my husband had all thrown in the towel. Though they are noble men, none of them were noble enough to choose the rights of their wives over the demands of a decaying society.

154

Forgiveness

As a Buddhist, I learned Metta meditation, the cultivation of benevolence or good will. The Hindus and the Buddhists have a universal prayer that states, "May all beings be well and happy." It sounds peaceful, and the literal meaning made me feel proud to be a Buddhist. Reality struck home when I started practicing Metta. I realized I could say that I loved my friends, family, and even strangers easily, but when it came to loving my enemies, I struggled. I convinced myself that if I could love them I could set them and myself free. It took me years to master this art. The last part was the most challenging because first I had to love myself.

As a student of Huna, an ancient practice from Hawaii, I learned Ho'oponopono, as taught by Morna Simione. It is the forgiveness ritual of Hawaiians. Practicing Ho'oponopono every day helps me be a better parent and therapist, the two most demanding roles of my life.

Liberation

After I had left my childhood home to earn a living, every Saturday morning I would wake up, set the water on to boil for tea, pick up the phone, and call my mother. "Hello, *Mā!* How are you?" "I am alive" was her constant response for twenty years. In 2009 my mother passed away as my brother, father, and I held her. It was the day of *Vaikunth Ekādashi,* which comes once every three years. *Vaikunth* is the celestial abode of Vishnu, the sustainer of the Universe, according to the Hindus. They believe that when someone crosses over on this day, the soul returns to source never to be reborn on any plane ever again. My mother lived a perfect life, dying at the age of seventy-eight, a perfect number for the Hindus. Coincidentally there are seventy-eight verses in the eighteenth and last chapter of the Bhagavad Gita.

After my mother's final rites were finished, I returned home to Ventura, California, with her mortal remains. The next morning I came down to my kitchen, set the water on to boil for tea, and looked at the same telephone. I heard my mother's voice reverberate within me, "I am alive*!"Ah! Maya! Mother of all illusion, or is it my truth?* Whenever thoughts of my mother cross my mind, I hear the words "I am alive." I know that love lasts beyond earthly life. Love keeps us eternally alive.

Conclusion

Whether it is your career, health, or relationships, when you find yourself struggling, I want you to sit with your pain as I did, as it's trying to tell you something. Your pain is a result of the conversations between your inner child, your inner critic, and your ego. Through all the muck of the past it can be hard to see the purpose behind your pain. For example, when you stir muddy water in a glass jar, it is hard to see through. But when you allow the jar to stand for a while, the dirt slowly settles and the water keeps getting clearer. Similarly, when you sit still, your emotions settle with time and you gain clarity in your thoughts. In this stillness you find your silent center – the seat of your power. This is where peace lives.

Through understanding and acceptance, it is easier to forgive, find peace, and experience love. Success is stopping the suffering. It is not an accident; it is a continuous, conscious journey. Living a liberated life comes from continuously being grateful for every gift you receive, no matter in what type of package it arrives.

When you make an effort, it is okay to have certain expectations from life. Liberation comes from remaining compassionately detached from all expectations.

"There is no way to happiness. Happiness is the way."
– The Buddha

I suggest that you write this phrase in your journal every night before bed:

"Just for today I let go of my worries. Just for today I shall be happy."

This is making daily deposits into your emotional bank. During your sleep time, you reprogram your subconscious, slowly but surely. When you change the way you think, you change the way you feel. Life becomes pleasurable and meaningful. So smile and be happy.

For now, I offer you my love and wish you a liberated life.

Namaste!

Keya Murthy, BSc, MS, CHt, resident Soul Coach of www.CoachKeya.com, derives great satisfaction from assisting entrepreneurs in achieving their breakthroughs and goals with grace and ease. She is certified as a clinical hypnotherapist, trainer in neuro-linguistic programming (NLP), Reiki Master, EFT practitioner, and Huna practitioner. Keya helps her clients become magicians in their own lives and a miracle in someone else's. Visit www.CoachKeya.com to receive a FREE discovery session for a pain-free life.

Forgiveness Is the Key to Healing

Susanne Romo

I WAS AFRAID MY ENTIRE CHILDHOOD.

My parents slept in separate bedrooms; my mother's bedroom was locked and barricaded from the inside. She was an alcoholic and a paranoid schizophrenic who tried to smother me when I was four. That was the first time I saw my mother put in a strait-jacket. She repeatedly told me, "I wish you had never been born. I should have had an abortion. I wish I had flushed you down the toilet."

I slept in my father's bed until I had my period at age eleven. I remember my mother attacking my father with a kitchen knife and being put once again into a strait-jacket. I watched one of my three brothers stab another one in my bedroom. I can still see the blood spurting from his leg, making rivulets down the red cherub-flocked wallpaper; can still hear my mother screaming and see the paramedics working to save his life. He walked in an entire-leg cast that summer, and one day my sister deliberately jumped on him as he lay on the sofa, which sent him back to the hospital.

I remember another alcoholic, drug-addled brother breaking down the front door in an angry rage. I used to walk to high school while my younger sister drove past me in the car our father had bought for her, honking the horn and laughing at me. My two older brothers were arrested for selling marijuana at a rock concert, and since my father was a parole officer, he was able to negotiate with the arresting officers to get them out of jail. He then paid to get them into rehabilitation.

My father pushed me to become a National Merit Scholar, take advanced classes, and attend summer school, but then refused to send me to college. Yet he paid for my younger sister, an average student at best, to further her education. He loved to promise things and not deliver. I learned not to trust men.

My mother and grandmother would be screaming curses at each other, but when the phone rang my mother would answer with a chirpy "Hello?" as if nothing was amiss. I never knew which mother I was coming home to after school. Would she be the sweater-knitting-and-cupcake-baking mother, or the antipsychotic-drug-addled mother who used the walls to support herself as she walked from room to room?

All this wasn't happening in a stereotypical broken home or bad neighborhood. We lived in upper-middle-class suburbia with white picket fences, Mercedes Benzes in the driveways, swimming pools, tennis courts, and horses. The sort of neighborhood where nothing bad happens. The kind of neighborhood where the Brady Bunch might have lived. A neighborhood where your parents loved you, your mother cooked nutritious meals and joined the PTA, and your father didn't kill your pets because he liked to see things die... while he forced you to watch.

We looked normal on the outside. It was only when you opened the front door and entered that the nightmare began.

I didn't understand love, and I didn't trust the world. When the two people who are supposed to love you unconditionally are monsters who show pleasant faces to the world, you learn very quickly that the world is not a safe place.

I learned that safety lay in invisibility. I was a very compliant child. I played by the rules, colored within the lines, shared my toys, and finished my homework without being asked. I hoped that if I just did everything the right way my parents might love me. In reality there was nothing I could ever do to make them love me.

Fast-forward to my workplace. Anger simmered inside me. This hidden rage served me well. It pushed me to become very successful career-wise. But it was eating me up inside. Anger was an insidious poison rotting my soul. I didn't believe in myself, but had learned how to put on a pleasant social mask. I laughed and went dancing. I dated every man who asked, and slept with any man who said "I love you." I dated men who were emotionally abusive because I was desperate to be loved and that was the only relationship pattern I knew.

I met my husband, Ernie, in 1990 while we were finishing our business administration degrees. We became friends as we negotiated the vast amount of schoolwork we had to do in the classes we shared. But I wasn't interested in him as a lover. I was twenty-five and finishing my degree; he was forty-six and returning to school. That twenty-one-year age gap bothered me. I also didn't trust that there was a man out there who was as truly good as he seemed to be. I understood sexual need; what I didn't understand was being touched with love and affection. Ernie was different. He was patient and kind. He scared me in a way no one else ever had. I wasn't sure whether I would destroy him with my poison or he would destroy me with his kindness.

He listened to me cry at night when my abusive boyfriends hurt me. He was there when I was overwhelmed dealing with my family. I tried for three years to get him to leave, but he didn't. He stuck with me. I truly believe now that he is an angel who was sent to save me. One day I looked at him and thought, "You are looking at the kindest person you will ever know. Give him and yourself a chance."

1995 was a critical year. Ernie and I married in October, and the next month my mother died. She had cut me out of her will because my sister told her I was plotting with my father to kill her. At her funeral I watched my siblings fighting about their inheritance, the stabbing, their hatred of each other, and the way I dressed my mother. (My sister claimed I had put her in her "drunk dress." I told her she should have been there when the funeral arrangements were being made.) I made the decision right then that I could no longer be connected to my family; that they would kill me with their poison. People who come from loving families cannot understand how leaving my family was one of the best decisions I have ever made in my life. I would never have been able to become the positive, forgiving, hopeful person I am today if I had not walked away from them.

Ernie knew I was unhappy, but he didn't know about the rage that boiled inside me. My mother's death opened a wound in my soul that I was terrified I would never be able to seal shut. I broke down emotionally. Poor man; he thought he had married a vivacious go-getter, and a month later she fell apart. But he still didn't give up on me.

Ernie gently steered me towards therapy. My psychiatrist suggested I take antidepressants. I told her that my fear was that if I took antidepressants it would mean I was crazy just like my mother. She smiled at me and said, "If you were diabetic, would you take insulin?" "Of course!" I replied. "Well, you have a disease, and it's caused by an imbalance of serotonin. I'm just asking you to take the medicine that will give you the ability to be at the starting gate of life with everyone else instead of having to come from behind. Depression is not a moral failing; it's just a chemical imbalance."

I started taking antidepressants. I was afraid they would dope me up like my mother's meds had, but I found that they quieted the rage inside me and gave me the emotional breathing room I needed to heal. They gave me the ability to react in a way that was better for me and for everyone around me. I also started therapy, and my pain poured out in torrents. I learned that my rage was actually suppressed grief.

I started reading books on healing and began journaling, putting my feelings down on the page. I found that writing let the poison ooze out of me. My soul, once a gaping black hole of rage, started to fill with hints of happiness. I learned that there was no memory inside me I needed to fear. I had already survived hell and now I learned how to heal. I was ready for the emotional warrior work ahead.

I learned that the healing journey is like peeling an onion. The thick, tough, outer layer is the hardest to crack. It's there to protect against the assaults the world throws at us. I learned as I peeled away the layers of painful memories from my soul that you do a lot of crying, but that the healing process gets easier with each layer removed. My healing journey wasn't easy, and it didn't happen quickly or in a linear path. There were times I thought I had gotten over a memory only to have something new trigger the pain years later; however, because I had done the prior healing work, I had created a new, stronger foundation that made subsequent healing happen faster and more easily. And like an onion, the inner layers get thinner, smaller, and easier to work with.

I learned about the power of forgiveness. Forgiveness was not a popular idea with me. Why should I forgive my father for abusing me? Why should I forgive my mother for trying to kill me and telling me my entire life that she wished I had never been born? Why did they deserve forgiveness? What I learned was that you don't forgive people for them; you forgive them for yourself. Forgiveness is the sweetest healing elixir that exists. As I forgave them, my heart lightened. Forgiveness gave me peace. Forgiveness is one of the most difficult things you will ever do, yet it is the best gift you will ever give yourself.

I still struggle with depression. There are dark days when I quarantine myself, take my extra meds, and wait for the day to pass. On those days I hate myself and tell myself I'm a worthless loser. Those are hard days. But I have learned that they will pass and that I just need to ride out the storm in my head.

Healing is not an easy process. As you heal you are able to look back at a memory almost as if it were a movie that happened to someone else. You learn to trust that those memories won't affect your psyche, and that is your win. I will always be "at the effect" of what happened to me. I will never be a woman who did not suffer from child abuse. The memories will always be there. But it's what I choose to do with my life that matters moving forward.

I wish you the best on your own healing journey.

Susanne Romo is a resilient survivor of child abuse. She writes positively about the painful subjects of anger, depression, and mental illness, and about the healing process, at www.HealingJourneyBlog. com and in her forthcoming book, *Pieces of Me: How Forgiveness Mended a Shattered Soul,* at www.HealingJourneyBlog.com. Susanne teaches women how to create vibrant, joyful lives of their choosing through the power of forgiveness. She is married to her best friend and they are the guardians of three rescue dogs and one rescue cat.

c2—

Unmasking Your Soul

Eileen Santos

You are here because your soul is calling you to embrace the REAL YOU!

IF YOU ARE READING THESE WORDS THEN YOU know without a doubt that there is a yearning deep inside you to live a more soulfully driven life. You are here because, like me, you are ready to transform your life; unmask your soul. I lived most of my life wearing a mask – a mask that was based in fear of being ME.

How is it that you come to live a life that doesn't feel completely fulfilling? In my case I spent most of my life pretending to be someone I wasn't because I was afraid of being judged, and I yearned to be accepted and loved by others. But in 2003, at the age of thirty-eight, something happened that changed my life forever. I had a dream, but not just any dream. This one was mystical and powerful. It was the first time I heard God's voice, loud and clear. It went like this:

I'm in an elevator in a tall office building, a skyscraper, with three other women. As the elevator descends, suddenly the cable breaks loose. The elevator begins to travel so rapidly it makes a hole in the side of the building and lands on a muddy, dark river of emotional turmoil. The elevator begins to skid on its back over the top of the river, with doors open to the sky. As I look towards the bank of the river, I see a woman in white robes with blond hair — she's my guardian angel. She reaches down into the elevator and pulls me to safety. As I get myself together, I notice that I've lost my wedding ring. I search high and low, and even ask a security guard who appeared in the dream to help me find it, but to no avail. As I wrestle with anxiety and emotion, I hear this strong, calming voice; God's voice. "My child," He says, "I have a mission for you. One that you won't understand right now, but be patient for in time all will be revealed to you."

As I woke up from this dream there was no mistaking what course of action I had to take. You see, up until that point I had been living a life full of lies. I was wearing a mask — several in fact. There had been so many signs that something was dreadfully wrong in my life, but I ignored them all. At the time I was employed as a marketing executive for a small student loan company, and I spent mindless days of endlessly working. I had become a workaholic to avoid the truth of what was waiting for me at home — a verbally abusive husband.

To most people I seemed very successful and happy, but the truth is that inside I was a mess. I had lived most of my life pleasing others, doing what I thought was expected of me, and not really listening to the yearning of my soul, which was asking for a happier, more loving, and healthier life. As I worked to meet the demands of my outer world, I had unknowingly closed myself off from my inner world, from my connection to spirit — to the divine which had always been very strong in my adolescence.

This dream unleashed a chain of events that changed me forever. I began to remember something very painful from my childhood that I had conveniently "forgotten." I had visions of being sexually abused at the age of four by a cousin whom I had trusted. He was an amazing artist and had always inspired my creative expression, but there was this side of him that had violated my deepest trust. In the darkness he

166

would whisper, "It's okay, don't be afraid." For years I was afraid of the dark and couldn't understand why until that moment.

My body was overwhelmed with all that was going on. Between the memories of the sexual abuse and the verbal abuse I was experiencing at home, my body went into overload. I began having fainting spells (a sign of my consciousness wanting to awaken), and yet when I went to doctors they couldn't find a medical condition for what I was experiencing. All the chaos (reminiscent of the muddy waters in the dream) in my outer world was just a reflection of the turmoil and pain I had been carrying for so long.

The epiphany had come in the form of that vivid dream. The universe was yelling loud and clear, "Wake up, Eileen. It's time for you to wake up from your stupor." And wake up I did. Immediately I knew this was a direct sign from God that I needed to change my life and step into my power. Shortly thereafter I separated from my husband. While the ending of this relationship turned out to be more difficult than I imagined, I found a new spark of faith and light within me – a spiritual awakening that transformed me forever.

"Why me?" I asked God the day He told me He had a mission for me. Somehow I had forgotten that my soul had volunteered for this task. I had conveniently forgotten that before I arrived at that point I had made a commitment to share my gifts with the world. Why? Because it was easier to forget than to courageously embrace the uncertainty of being ME. But despite my fear and feelings of being overwhelmed, I found the inner strength to embrace my divinity and witness the divinely orchestrated unmasking of each chamber of my soul.

With each passing day I discovered soulful gifts that had been dormant since my childhood. Art was the first to emerge. No surprise that the first pastel I was guided to paint was of my own awakening and was called *Spiritual Awakening.* I remember loving art so much as a child, but I never gave myself permission to follow this passion. I was too busy living my life for others rather than living it for ME. Then other creative expressions began to emerge: songwriting and singing, poetry, and writing. I had been giving my power away to others for so long that I had trouble speaking my truth and really using my voice as God intended. It was no coincidence that I was being guided to sing so I could heal that part of me that I had shut down for so long for fear of not being loved or accepted.

Then the universe began to send new people into my life, people who would contribute to my spiritual growth. One of these happened to be an accountant turned energy healer. I could relate to him because I had lived most of my life in the corporate world, too; first as an engineer, then as a consultant, and then as a marketing executive. It was no coincidence that I met this energy healer.

I became so fond of his work that I decided to take one of his meditation classes. And that's when a perfect stranger taking the same class came up to me and said, "Do you know you're meant to be a healer?" I didn't know what to say. This wasn't something I'd expected to hear.

As all of my hidden treasures began to emerge, I also discovered that TRUE LOVE sometimes shows up in our lives when we least expect it and in packages that can challenge us to our core. When I began to seek counsel from friends and family to support me through these major life changes, I unexpectedly met my twin soul. It was so powerful, yet challenging at the same time because she was a woman. This was against everything I had been raised to believe was acceptable.

What made this relationship so different was the instant kinship and soul connection I felt in her presence. It was like we had known each other forever, beyond time and space. But as the closeness grew, I realized I was feeling more than gratitude and friendship; I was feeling deep, profound love. This love was deeper than any love I had experienced to that point. I immediately resisted the feelings. How could this be? How could I be in love with a woman? That was not the way I had imagined my life. The truth is I was more concerned about what my family and others would say than about how I was really feeling. At that point I still didn't love myself enough to know that once again I was giving my power away to others. This was my decision to make, yet I was afraid to lose those I loved the most. I had grown up in a Catholic, Puerto Rican household, and all I could think about was how my mother was going to react.

But just as quickly as the divine challenged what I believed to be acceptable in my life, it provided me with the experiences to gain greater clarity of my TRUTH. The divine helped me understand that this type of sacred love chooses you, you don't choose it. Despite the package being different than what I imagined (gender in my case, but it can come in any form – age, religion, etc.), this kind of love has its own soul language and is an unstoppable force that is divinely orchestrated. And with that realization, I was able to accept it without guilt or shame and receive it as a sacred gift from the universe.

And from my own transformational journey of the last twelve years emerged the Unmasking Your Soul Blueprint™. I didn't realize it at the time, but the divine was deliberately taking me through my own healing and transformation so I could share this teaching with YOU.

The Unmasking Your Soul Blueprint is built on a foundation of three key stages: Truth, Light, and Healing. Each stage helps you connect more deeply with an aspect of you that has been hidden, masked, or forgotten, so that you can heal and transform that part of you to its original form of wholeness and completeness. As you immerse yourself in the divine teachings of this process, you emerge as the REAL YOU.

These were the words given to me by the divine to describe each stage:

- **Truth:** To begin the healing process, you must accept and awaken to the truth within your soul. Accepting the truth is a journey of self-discovery in which you begin to UNMASK

169

those areas of your life that are still keeping you from expressing your most authentic you.

- **Light:** As you experience this awakening and pierce the spiritual veil, you shift from a sense of separateness to one of connectedness. As you CONNECT with your authentic you – your divine light – you begin to shed the hurts and ego-driven behaviors that no longer serve you.
- **Healing:** As you fully EMBODY your divine expression, you unlock your soul's DNA and begin living a more joyful, passionate, inspired, and soul-driven life.

No matter what has happened to you, I'm here to tell you that you can transcend it. If I was able to break free from my old life, you can, too. Listen to your soul's yearning in this moment and see where it takes you. Start your journey of transformation today and begin unmasking your soul. Remember, the first step is TRUTH. Go within, seek your truth, and take the first step to embracing who you really are and embodying your soul's desire. From there you will birth your true purpose in life.

I invite you to go on a transformational journey with me in my forthcoming book, *Unmasking Your Soul: A Transformational Journey of Truth, Light, and Healing.* In the book I go deeper into each stage and include poetry, art, meditative activations, divine teachings, and journaling exercises to help you transform your own life. If you would like to be the first to know about its release, sign up at the URL below.

Eileen Santos is an interfaith minister whose mission is to work as an energy healer, artist, and transformational leader for those seeking to live a more soul-driven life. Dedicated to bringing healing and wholeness to her clients, she helps them remember the infinite-loving, divine beings they truly are. Her book *Unmasking Your Soul* is planned for release in 2015. For information on the book, visit www.UnmaskingYourSoul.com. For information about Eileen's products and services, visit www.PortraitsOfYourSoul.com.

~~

Put an End to Running on Empty: Bringing Back Balance for Over-Givers

Helen M. Sherry, PhD

HOW WOULD YOU LIKE TO EASILY CREATE a beautiful, living vision board that reminds you daily of your desires and goals and reflects your current state – a vibrant, organic anchor for your dreams, reminding you to stay in balance? I would love to share my story of how I created my Living Dream Gardens and finally moved past a lifetime of depletion from over-giving into a joy-filled life of balance.

If you're like me, you've often found yourself prioritizing everyone else's needs above your own. I honor you for your caring heart that wants to give your best to others, but the reality is that if you're not recharging yourself daily, you're probably running on empty. My life lesson was that you can end up broken by nurturing others without filling yourself up first.

I learned to create balance in my life and want to share my experience to help you also put an end to the cycle of over-giving.

For me, the concept that others come first was ingrained early on. As the eldest of five children, I most often felt my harried mom's approval and love when I lent a hand with my siblings. My young mind decided that caregiving was crucial in order to matter.

On top of that, the mantra of my beloved but very busy father was that we are on Earth to serve those who have less. He was a successful businessman who devoted many nights and weekends to helping others. "Yes" was his default option, and for too many years it was mine. I always knew he loved me, but he wasn't around much. Mom would fix dinner, putting his into a special warming drawer because we never knew when he'd be home. In order to see his smiling face, I went with him, assisting whenever I was allowed. His causes became mine. I sent my allowance to orphans, and sat with him at candlelit prayer vigils to feel close to him.

Both Mom and Dad taught me "Work First – Play Last," which translated to "Work First – Play Rarely." That served me in grad school, but not so well later on.

Fast-forward to my deeply rewarding career as a licensed psychotherapist for over thirty years and as a Military and Family Life Counselor (MFLC) since 2009 helping our troops and their families on military bases around the world. I love my work, but had no concept of prioritizing myself along with those I served.

After so many years of running on empty, I've finally seen the impact of my early imprints. With the help of my Living Dream Gardens, I'm letting them go forever.

I wish it had not taken several short-lived marriages and debilitating back pain to get me to wake up and put an end to this cycle of imbalance. But then again, that's what helped me commit to my true passion.

What is my true passion besides helping others? It's sharing my Living Dream Gardens. A Living Dream Garden is something I developed that combines my love of nature, metaphysics, and spirituality, along with the power of symbolism that I discovered when I studied Sandplay Therapy in Switzerland for six months. Through weekly seminars with Dora Kalff and lectures at the Jung Institute,

I learned about the ability of symbols to evoke change. In my own Sandplay Therapy with Dora, I experienced profound healing of the pain of my broken relationships as I placed tiny figurines of personally meaningful symbols into miniature worlds that I created in the sand.

Spirit gave me the inspiration to create my Living Dream Gardens in 2006. It was a magical "aha" moment as I got a vision of interweaving the complex strands of my life and my love of symbols with succulents, crystals, and power animals into beautiful, living creations. I realized that all these elements I loved could synergistically combine into a powerful "healing garden."

Later, as I learned about the Law of Attraction, I realized that I had created an "intention garden" – a living vision board. My tiny Garden packed with all things precious to me has lived on my bedroom altar ever since. It serves as a daily reminder that I matter – that I need to take care of ME before I can pass along my healing energies to others.

My healing journey continued. The following year during my preparation to become a Native American Quested Elder, I was given the assignment to create a medicine wheel on paper, incorporating the Four Directions. I expanded this into a large medicine wheel Dream Garden in my backyard. Meditating with my outdoor Garden opened me to see for the first time that my dad had meant service to others, not self-sacrifice. At my Elderhood Initiation, I committed to balancing giving and receiving; my vow was to give from a place of full, not empty.

Yet as clear as that commitment felt at the time, unhealthy old patterns spidered back, drawing me into the web of compulsive giving. As a result of letting that happen, I ended up having injury after injury. Eventually my wise body knocked me on my behind one last time, causing the need for emergency back surgery and the opportunity to break those patterns at a much deeper level.

During this time of physical pain, it seemed my Dream Gardens mimicked my physical state. Ants and snails devoured my outside Garden, and mealy bugs destroyed my little container Dream Garden inside. I tried rebuilding both in hopes of solidifying my personal commitment to change, but the changes didn't last for more than a few days.

My body screamed at me to slow down and take care of myself. In desperation I prayed I would "get it" so I could end this pattern and enjoy a pain-free, joy-filled life.

Then it happened! In the midst of post-op pain, I remembered that I am a healer, and "got" that I was the one I needed to heal. I limped outdoors in my pajamas to create a bedside healing Garden, and embarked on a year of living differently, leaning into joy. I started a daily before-work practice of meditating, connecting with my Dream Gardens, and writing.

It's embarrassing to admit that several months after surgery I relapsed back into over-doing and under-being. As soon as I started feeling better, I forgot my commitment to myself and started fitting in more clients; my self-worth since childhood has been so closely tied to feeling needed. Instead of my daily practice (and despite my husband's chiding,) I found myself rushing to the office, rotating ice packs, and fidgeting in my therapist's chair to find a comfortable position to support my aching back.

I sensed it was coming – the final wakeup call asking me to really get it for good. Yet I couldn't break the pattern until I needed to travel to New Zealand to morally support my husband and his terminally ill mother. The neurosurgeon advised against the trip, but by riding through airports in a wheelchair, I did it.

A gray cloud of sadness swallowed me as I sat in a wheelchair for the first time. Out of that despair and pain came the unshakable commitment I now honor to stay in balance. I've figured out that my back is my barometer, and if it's hurting, I've slipped into running on empty. I'm amazed that as soon as I stop and refill, I am out of pain, and life becomes fun again.

My Living Dream Gardens are the best way I know to recharge, raising my vibration daily. I feel pure joy as I watch the succulents grow and bloom, and I'm enveloped by a sense of peace as I link to Source in prayer, supported by the healing energies of my Gardens. There's a 12-Step saying: "It works when you work it and you're worth it." I had to decide once and for all that I was worth it.

My Living Dream Gardens help me each day to stay balanced. They give me something alive and beautiful to tend so I can be reminded of my own aliveness and beauty, and of the importance of slowing down and taking care of me.

From all these experiences, I've learned three things:

1. You really DO matter just as much as everyone else.
2. It takes dedication, effort, and focus to stay on a path of self-love.
3. Creating a Living Dream Garden is a powerful step in the direction of self-care.

I'd like to now share with you how to create and benefit from your own Living Dream Garden. It's a simple, relaxing, and fun way to tend to yourself. I'll give step-by-step instructions to create your Garden, but I've also created a special guided visualization to help you tap in to the power and feeling of your own Living Dream Garden. You can watch it now by going to my website, www.LiveandGrow.com/visualization.

Once you have your vision, the fun part comes next: creating your own Living Dream Garden! This practice is first about envisioning, and then manifesting into reality that which you desire. You're going to create your own 3D living and growing vision board.

Building Your Living Dream Garden

Step 1: Assembling.
- Container with a hole in the bottom – preferably no more than 5" – 6" deep

- Cactus planting mix and Perlite
- Small stones – to fill the bottom of your planter
- Stones for natural features – mountains, mesas, caves, or cliffs. Find or create different shapes.
- Crystals – choose from a local metaphysical shop or online
- Succulents (not cacti) – in an array of shapes, colors, and heights, several of each to unify the landscape. Ask your nursery or home center for easy growers.
- Power animals – 1 or 2 small animal figurines that you saw in your visualization. Dollar stores are great for these.
- Spiritual figurines – you can find small figurines and angels at your local metaphysical store or online.
- Symbols – choose a few representing what you wish to create in your ideal life (such as a bluebird of happiness), or reminding you to play (a mini dancing shoe, ice skate, tennis racquet). Check out craft stores.

I want to share a quick story about the power of symbols. One day after a spinal decompression treatment, I took my dog to the park, spotted a beautiful tree, and felt the urge to climb. As a child, climbing trees was one of my greatest joys. Now, at my age and with the back issues I've had, it didn't seem realistic. Yet I did it! God knows what my chiropractor would have said, but I felt truly happy up in that tree. Then it dawned on me: the tall succulents in my Living Dream Gardens look like trees! That symbol reinforces my desire to have fun again, so choose your symbols purposefully.

- Spritzer bottle of distilled water

Step 2: Creating.

Layer stones in the bottom of the planter, then fill 2/3 with cactus mix. Place stones for natural features towards the back of the planter. Arrange the succulents, then more mix. Add your crystals, power animals, symbols, etc. Rearrange until it feels right. Sprinkle with Perlite.

Step 3: Watering.

Water thoroughly until it runs out the bottom. Thereafter, spritz 1–2 times weekly. With succulents, less (water and care) is more. In the growing season, add fertilizer to your distilled water.

Step 4: Placing.

Set in a bright window and say a prayer, focusing on joyfully manifesting your dreams.

Step 5: Connecting.

Each day BEFORE you go out into the world to serve others, prayerfully connect to your Garden, asking for the blessing of Spirit on your intentions. As you care for your Garden, it will grow, just like your dreams.

As you change, allow your Garden to grow and evolve with you. Add new symbols, crystals, and succulents. Have fun with it. Play and enjoy. Live and grow and thrive. You're worth it!

Helen Sherry, PhD, is a gifted intuitive with an affinity to all things living. The creator of Living Dream Gardens (living vision boards), she synergistically blends Native American wisdom and medicine animals, deity figurines, crystals, and symbols with life-giving succulents to create personalized works of art to help people manifest their dreams. She's an author and licensed psychotherapist, practicing in Arroyo Grande, California, and also serving military families around the globe. Her website is www.LiveandGrow.com.

From Brown Bird to Yellow Bird: Healing the Hurts that Clutter One's Heart

Julie Stamper

IF YOU ARE LIKE MOST OF US WHO WALK the path of transformation, you yearn for that magic moment when an idea or attitude that is not serving you well is suddenly seen with clarity and new understanding. That "aha" moment makes it easy to discard what is not working and retain what is true. Some spend years in therapy to gain that sort of inner knowingness. I am proposing a do-it-yourself meditation experience that has served me well on many days and helped me get through a variety of conundrums. After all, the journey of transformation evolves one step at a time. Sometimes it is the simplest of limiting beliefs that holds us back from experiencing our greatness.

My story begins with an awareness that I often refer to myself as a little brown bird. This image best describes how I feel when I am in an uncomfortable situation or feel that it is best to play small or go unnoticed. There is some degree of comfort in being a little brown bird. These little messengers do entertain me as they flit about from branch to branch, avoiding the bigger, flashier, or more powerful birds.

When I was deep in the middle of my career as a teacher and counselor, I never felt like a little brown bird. I had purpose and vision. After I retired and moved away from my comfortable surroundings, I began to doubt myself. I didn't quite fit in with my new town, and I didn't feel free to express myself without some form of social reprisal. "Go along to get along" was not my style, yet there I was, doing just that. Life as a little brown bird was becoming ever more stifling, and I wanted to spend my next chapter in life as my true uncensored self.

Since New Year's Day, 2014, I have been on a mission to clear family and social programming that is not in alignment with where I want to go in my life. My limiting beliefs about money and abundance are another kettle of fish, derived from social norms rooted in outdated paradigms. My goal was to engage the Universe in helping me vibrate on a higher level. I was ready to be all that I could be. Continuing as a little brown bird just wasn't going to cut it.

One summer day while gardening, I became especially inspired by my surroundings. The flower garden was buzzing with life and glowing with color. I sat down to meditate amid this beauty and asked my spirit guide, Anastasia, to show me something I needed to know. As we looked about the garden and appreciated all there was to enjoy, she reminded me that I needed to be anchored in nature's beauty to feel whole. The next step in my meditation involved Anastasia reaching into my heart and drawing out something that I needed to see. She reached in and out came a little brown bird. I was encouraged to review a story from my life that the bird represented. As the story was completed, the bird began to alter itself, turning into a yellow evening grosbeak before flying away.

Several little brown birds were removed from my heart that day, and I have continued to do this meditation whenever it feels like I need a clearing of dense energy. These little brown birds, and what they represent, were taking up room in my heart and had to be released in order for me to realize my desire to vibrate at a higher level. It is amazing how much lighter a person can feel when there is less clutter in one's heart. I believe that we all have a need to make room in our hearts, BUT we need to clear out the old to make way for the new.

What did the little brown birds represent?

The fear that I am not enough

An example of this fear came to me as the story of my seventh grade self. I loved staying after school to do my gymnastics routine, and I would often come home and continue to do my passes in the family room. The room was long and skinny, perfect for cartwheels and leaping about. One day my dad was trying to watch TV and there I was scampering back and forth in my own little world. At one point when he was particularly annoyed, he muttered under his breath, "You look like a cow." Teenage girls do not have a thick enough skin to brush off a comment like that, so I stopped practicing when Dad was home.

When it came time for the city gymnastics meet, I surprisingly made the team, along with my best friend. She was the consummate athlete in my mind. She won every ribbon in track and field. I already knew that I wasn't a good enough athlete, but I was happy to have made the team. Dad would need to drive me to the meet and I dreaded that prospect. I asked him not to come in. I didn't want him to be embarrassed by watching his cow-like daughter in action.

As the winners were announced, my school was named and my friend hopped up. The only problem was that I had won the ribbon. This was completely embarrassing for me and for my friend. Now I felt horrible for her. When I climbed into our truck for the ride home, Dad asked how it went. I told him that I had won a blue ribbon; however, there was no joy in it. I was still a cow, and my friend was not happy either. When I got home I threw the ribbon away. I have shied away from competitive sports since that day.

Being duplicitous

This is an old family story that I am not proud of. I was five or six years old, and my little sister and I were sorting through some change. I tried to convince her to accept a nickel instead of a dime, arguing that the nickel was larger so therefore worth more. I was just old enough to know the value of the coins. My mother was furious. She let me know in no uncertain terms that it was never okay to take advantage of another.

The message to be quiet

I was not to speak up because I might say something that would embarrass others. When it came to expressing any emotion deemed negative, I was told I shouldn't feel that way. Therefore I learned my feelings were not correct or not particularly important in the larger scope of things. I learned to question whether my feelings were a collection of cues that I had somehow misread.

My fear of math skill deficiencies and how they connect to my unenlightened view of money

In the fifth grade I earned a D on a math test. My mother was livid. No child of hers was going to do so poorly. She marched me down the street to the dime store to buy flashcards and workbooks to get the problem solved ASAP. She lectured me about my poor performance the entire way to the store and on the way back. We got home to discover that there was not a bag to carry in, and that the items we had chosen in the store were still in our hands. We had walked out without paying for them.

The color drained out of Mom's face as she realized that we had stolen them! We had to hatch a plan to sneak back into the store, pretend to put the items back, reselect them, and then pay as usual. By the time it was all over we were both humiliated in our own ways. Two family rules had been breached: never steal, and never do anything less than your best.

After all the flashcard drills, I learned to dislike math and got the idea that I was not good at it. My mother's good intentions backfired and I still avoid math like the plague, even simple tasks like balancing my checkbook.

* * *

As grace would have it, my husband and I live in the forest, and birds are regular visitors. Lots of little brown birds, jays, and hummers come by. On occasion we are graced with beautiful evening grosbeaks. They are so distinctive with their bright yellow bodies and black and white markings. That summer we had up-close and personal visitations from the evening grosbeaks. They came in pairs and tried to take over our hummingbird feeders. The female would sit on the feeding tray with her wings wrapped around the juice bottle, with the male perched on top of the hanger that supports the feeder. Our tinted windows allowed us to see them up close, within inches, without their knowledge.

When I was studying with Native American teachers, they taught us that a critter only shows itself to you if it is sending you a message. My husband and I are always delighted to see the diversity of creatures that live in our forest, and we keep our copy of *Animal Speak* by Ted Andrews within easy reach in order to reference the meaning of each sighting. I was astonished to read that the primary energy of grosbeaks is the healing of the family heart. They teach us to heal old wounds and hurts of family origin. They ask us to see how the separate notes in their song make up the melody, just as the separate events in our lives create family patterns that continue to influence us later in life.

There were more evening grosbeaks in the summer of 2014 than ever before, and I now know that this was no accident. I was so happy to have these reminders of healing in my life. My stories are a testament to how an emotionally charged incident has a lasting effect, even if the incident was engineered to do good. Going from little brown bird to a beautiful evening grosbeak is quite a transformation. I now have more room in my heart to vibrate with the energy of abundance. I joyfully attend my zumba class without feeling like a cow. I am learning about money management because I know that I have the smarts to figure it out and make good decisions for me. I am grateful to my parents for all they taught me, and consider my lessons in forgiveness and abundance great blessings.

I'd now like to share with you the simple steps I take to do a daily meditation. (This meditation is my adaptation of a much longer version of Alecia Power's "How Your Spirit Tutor Awakens Your Power" webcast at www.AwakeningtoAbundance.com.)

Set an intention for the topic you would like to examine with a new sense of clarity.

Prepare yourself as you would for employing the meditation style you are familiar with in your daily practice.

Ask for help from any spirit guide or trusted spiritual entity you resonate with.

Ask to be shown something you need to know or be reminded of in order to anchor you in your life.

Ask the spirit guide to reach into your heart and show you something you need to know. This "thing" may not be a little brown bird; the imagery will be a personal representation or symbol that you will understand.

Ask for the story behind this symbol and what it has to teach you.

Once the lesson is complete, release the symbol and its story with love and light.

I hope that these seven steps will help you on your transformational journey! May your heart be light and open for new experiences that nurture your soul.

Julie Stamper, MA Ed., draws on thirty years of classroom teaching and counseling skills to move clients forward to discovering their authentic truth. She presents information succinctly, in an easy-to-follow format, merging storytelling and content that invites the explorer to embark upon the journey of personal growth. Readers will recognize themselves in the pages of her upcoming book, *Conversations with Money.* Visit Julie at www.JulieStamper.com, or on Facebook and LinkedIn.

Moving Out of the Darkness
by Divine Light

Jeanne Starkey

I'VE REACHED A PLACE WHERE THE ONLY way to move forward in my life is to take a journey backward and retrace my steps. So I'm shining Love's Light on my life experiences and transitions with the hope that by reading a part of my story, a light will begin to burn within your own heart and lead you to see any painful experiences of your own life in a new way and with Love's Light.

Some would say I'm on a recovery mission, but I like to think I'm on a mission of discovery. I am discovering what feels right to me now, while finding, reviewing, and processing what has been hidden beneath the story of my life.

I am questioning everything about myself. I'm doing my best not to be too hard on myself or push myself to move too fast through this process. Instead I am attempting to look at myself with a loving curiousness as I allow my Soul to extract the meaning and purpose of the path I have traveled in life thus far. I am striving to have an open heart as I search for a self that has long been buried by the rubble created by my life's unfolding. I'm also listening to what my Soul, my heart, my truest self if you will, would have me hear as I journey within to view my life in a new light, to heal, and to collect and claim the treasures waiting to be discovered.

The following is a glimpse into the process that my Soul and Divine Love are leading me through in order to discover my buried self. The writing of this story is a gift and tool inspired by Spirit for me to process my inner work and express it to the world. I am honored for you to share in the process as it is unfolding.

A Story of Healing: The Healing Begins

I found myself buried alive at the base of my heart's stairwell. Encompassed in the darkness, I cried out for meaning for all I had experienced in my life. I longed for relief from the fear, angst, and depression that was threatening the life of my Soul. I wanted to be rescued and my Soul to be set free. Not knowing how to accomplish this, I pleaded, cried, and begged God for help. I wallowed in self-pity and denial, reliving the same traumas of my life over and over again in my mind. Trying to get over myself only landed me deeper in the darkness.

Then a Light of Divine Love shone at the base of my heart. It was so powerful that it was too much for me to accept at first. I denied my worthiness of it and my ability to harness its power. I knew instinctively that I would have to use this light to find my way through the darkness of my heart in order to reclaim, recover, and even discover parts of myself that had been lost in the dark debris caused by my life's storms and transitions. I could hear the quiet whisper of my Soul saying, "You must be courageous. Shine the light into the darkness. Look closely at what scares and hurts you. Look with the Light of Love and see with new eyes your life in order to truly live and be free."

I finally chose to respond to my Soul's whisper and clutched onto the Light of Divine Love from Spirit like a lantern and began my walk into the darkness of my heart and up its stairwell into healing.

I took the first step up and was still encompassed by darkness, but I began to hear the cries of a very small child. I held the lantern of love out in front of me, hoping to find the child within the dark. I could feel her fear and hear her plea: "I don't want to die. I'm scared." I called out to her, "Come here into the light." I reached out my hand, pleading for her to grab hold of it. The ancient shadows within me held on to her tightly; they were reluctant to release her. I didn't have the words to give to this three-year-old aspect of myself to heal her, but I longed for her to know she was loved and valued. I reached my hand farther into the darkness and called to her once more. I felt her tiny hand grab hold of my fingertips as the shadows finally let her go. I cradled this beginning aspect of self in my heart. Still unsure of what was to come or how things were going to work out, I felt a sense of ease as I heard my Soul whisper, "All is well, all is well." I knew in that moment that I had reclaimed my innocence.

I took another step upwards, and as I did the Light of Divine Love now shone upon a five-year-old girl who lay crying in her mother's bed. I immediately recognized her and the pain within her welled up inside me. I felt her sense of helplessness and the worry she held inside over her inability to help her mother. Memories of lying with my mother at night while my father stayed out late drinking came rushing up into my mind's eye. I saw myself lying next to my mother in the dark as her cries and sorrows over him and other deeply held pain within her own heart spilled out of her and into my little ears. Her pain welled up inside my tiny heart as I lay helpless to make her heartache go away. I could do nothing to quell the anguish inside my mother other than to listen to her. I held up the lantern so the Light of Divine Love shone on that helpless child's face and I kissed her on the head. I told her she had done a beautiful job of being there for her mother. I told her she was a good listener and by doing just that she had given her mom a precious gift. I drew her up into myself, and in doing so I claimed my gift of listening with heart.

Just a few steps farther up and the Light of Divine Love illuminated enough space for me to find an ageless young girl sitting cross-legged and chained to a brown, tattered sofa. She was covered with scars and bruises and was so pale and fragile. I watched her from a distance. She sat with tears streaming down her face while she repeatedly pulled the links of chain through her fingers. First she'd let it collect in a pile in her lap until it became taut at the end of its origin, and then release it back the other way until she reached the clasp around her ankle. As I stood there watching, the clinking sound of the chain began to create a vibration deep within my chest, and then from out of the darkness the sound of my father's rage came rushing into my ears.

I was soon enveloped by the total remembrance of hours and sometimes entire days of being held captive on our living room sofa as my drunken father yelled, scolded, and lectured me on some misdeed I had done that warranted his reprimand. My full attention was required or the iron fingers of his hand would come cracking down on my head like a lead pipe. Over and over I heard about my shortcomings and the pain and trouble I had caused by whatever error I had made. Filled with remorse and sorrow I would vow to myself that I would be better. I would do better and never disappoint not just my father but anyone ever again. Once my father exhausted his anger and disappointment over me and my wrongdoings, I was then expected to stay put and bear witness to his rants of self-loathing as he paced the floor in front of me. His pain became mine, leaving me scarred and bruised from events in his life that my child's mind could never understand. My chest would feel so full and tight with angst, sadness, worry, and pain, yet I still managed to find room enough to cram in feelings of regret and guilt for somehow bringing the residual fallout from my father's emotional storms upon my mother, brother, and grandmother. We all had to weather these storms to some degree; I just hated to be the one who fueled them.

My hand tightly gripped the lantern of Divine Light as I moved myself forward with its glow to come and sit next to the part of myself that had been left alone, chained to that sofa. I set the lantern down before us and embraced the child as she laid her tear-stained face against my chest. We sat together in silence, in the glow of the Light of Divine Love, and let all the tightness within our chests dissipate into the glow that now surrounded us. Together we were filled with a sorrow, as well as a deep love for my father. We shared compassion for his pain and suffering as we worked to shed light and understanding upon the demons within him that he tried so hard to keep buried and controlled by the use of alcohol. Love and forgiveness for my father swirled around us as we both let go of the hurt his emotional storms had inflicted. The process of letting go and forgiveness was enough to release the ageless child from her captive state; the chains that had once kept her bound had vanished. Her scars and bruises still remained, but she now had color in her face and was free to move forward into healing. I knew she required more time to heal, but she now had enough strength to take my hand as we moved one more step up and into healing within the stairwell of my heart. I had claimed my ability to forgive with unconditional love.

By my willingness to write my story of healing as guided by Spirit, I'm gaining freedom from constricted shadow-perspectives of my inner child and transforming my suffering into useable aspects while gaining a clearer awareness of my current self. I once heard author Elizabeth Gilbert say, "Failure, disaster, shame, suffering, and pain do not necessarily make you a better person unless you participate in turning it into something good. Never waste your suffering. Suffering without catharsis is nothing but wasted pain."

Since writing this story, I have done a bit of research on the subject of "inner-child healing" and have come to learn that this type of work is not just healing for the individual doing the work, but also healing for numberless generations of their ancestors and descendants.

Through my process of writing and opening myself to the guidance provided by Spirit, I have been able to view, understand, and bring healing and light to some of the suffering my parents experienced along with my own. My love for them is endless, as I know theirs is for me.

As I write these words I am still participating in the healing process with Spirit and continue to shine the Light of Divine Love at my life's experiences so I can continue to heal and ascend the stairwell of my own heart. I want to thank you, the reader, for traveling this far with me in my transformational process and for sharing in part of my healing. My deepest wish is that anyone who suffers or feels constricted by painful life experiences will take time and allow the Light of Divine Love to shine within. Let it illuminate the dark spaces you may have and transform and heal them into the treasures that surely lie inside your own heart. Peace, Love, and Light.

Jeanne Starkey has passionately helped others by working within the healthcare and educational systems while raising her family. She cared for and supported her parents as they battled and passed away from cancer. At age forty-six she received her BA in elementary and special education. In 2012 she received her own cancer diagnosis and underwent treatment. She is currently working at viewing her life by a new light. To reach Jeanne, email her at JustStarJest@gmail.com.

Honoring Your Value: Adjusting Your Lens of Self-Perception

Kara Stoltenberg, MA, Ed.

In a moment, standing at my bedroom window, gazing out into nothing, I realized something that would forever change my life.

TO PAINT AN ACCURATE PICTURE OF THIS MOMENT, it is helpful to know some of the circumstances that were happening at that time. Let's just say that things hadn't exactly gone as I had hoped in my life. I was a single mom with a precious four-year-old boy, trying to do what was best for him. That was pretty much the goal of my life. I really couldn't see beyond that.

I was extremely critical of myself and at the time felt incapable of making good decisions. A loud voice in my head said, "If you make no more decisions, you cannot make a wrong one." Basically I didn't trust my judgment. I thought to myself, "If I just hold here, I can raise my son without totally ruining his life." That was *really* important to me. In every decision I made, I agonized over trying to consider what it would mean for him. I would even try to imagine how that one decision would play out over the course of his lifetime. (I now know that though I was well-intentioned in caring for his best interests, this way of thinking was irrational and obviously could not have helped me move forward!)

My own mom repeatedly and gently reminded me that I really needed to consider *my* well-being. She would say, "If it is good for you, it will be good for him." But I was operating in such self-denial and self-abandonment that I couldn't resonate with what she was saying. I had *no* idea how to consider myself. At the time I thought she just didn't understand what I was going through. I later realized that the problem with that way of thinking was that if I wasn't honoring my own best interests, I *couldn't* make good decisions.

I don't remember what decision I was facing at that time. What I do remember is a numb feeling; staring out through the glass, looking into the world on the other side, trying to find a connection to God. I felt alone and empty. I was frozen as I tried to move forward. I no longer trusted my instincts. I just didn't want to make any more mistakes. I had little faith in myself. I asked myself over and over, "Is this it?"

In that moment at the window, the message came straight to my heart. It was as simple as it was profound. "I am just as important to God as that little boy. To God, we are of the same importance. There is no ranking system in which he falls at the top and I am somewhere down at the bottom. *That precious child* is *not* of higher value than I am."

To God, we are equal.

Equally relevant.

Equally important.

Equally VALUABLE.

It was the first time that the essence of my value struck a chord that resonated in a way that I could hear it. I knew the great value of that little boy, but... *me?*

Like *that?*

Yes.
Me... like that.

The message came to me that simply, but I got it. I was able to receive this truth about myself, and in that instant I chose to believe it. Though I would have much to ponder and learn in the way of honoring this newly acquired truth, I decided right then to try to live from the perspective of my own personal value. It changed everything.

Prior to that moment I had made some pretty self-destructive decisions. I didn't mean to. In fact, that was as far from my intention as is possible; I just made decisions that were not in line with the core of who I am. I was so out of touch with my core essence that I couldn't even connect with my good and discerning judgment in making decisions. I was caught up in what I "should" do. (That is what happens when you forget your value.) I *thought* I was terrible at making good choices; clearly my life seemed a reflection of that. It had always been so easy for me to see and reflect other people's value, but I would readily dismiss my own. It was easy to stand up for others, and yet I was silent in regard to myself.

What I have learned is that I am actually really great at knowing in my gut what is the right course of action. I was, unfortunately, also good at denying what my gut said (aka: denying my value because I didn't stand true and honor who I was in major life decisions). This resulted in my doing what I thought I should do. I was doing whatever it took to keep others happy or to follow societal norms. What you should do also shows up as a distorted voice that tells you how lousy

197

you are and what you should do to make up for that fact. What you should do can show up as someone in your life telling you what to do and your following suit (because you should!) My decisions were very much in line with what I should do, not with what was right for me.

When I started considering my own value in determining the course of my life, I *stopped living in the energy of SHOULD.* The startling discovery was that "should" squandered my light! Not showing up and acknowledging my value, my very precious being, disconnected me from the Source of life. No wonder I felt suffocated and trapped, as if I could never really find my place. I felt obligated and controlled. I did *not* feel like I was aligned with my heart or living my soul purpose. Even the things in my life that were brilliant and beautiful could not be fully enjoyed.

When you are aligned with the belief of your VALUE and honoring yourself as the precious, created being that you are, your light shines brightly. Outside of that light it's pretty hard to make awesome decisions.

When you are connected to the value of who you are, you are acknowledging God. You are living in gratitude for the fact that you were created. It is this energy, the essence of your creation, that composes the truth of who you are. The things that you have been through are just experiences. They are circumstances. It is a mistake to look at yourself through the filter of what has happened in your life; to see your value through the filter of what you have or haven't been able to accomplish; to determine whether or not you are worth anything based on what you have to show for it. YOU ARE VALUABLE because you were born! You were designed. You are unique. You are the only one who can bring exactly what you have to the world.

The circumstances you have navigated have nothing to do with defining your value, but your triumph in them does reflect the incredible worth that you hold! When you can begin to accept the amazing person that you are, additionally evidenced by your survival of these circumstances, you begin to catch a glimpse of the truth. You are divinely beautiful! For a very long time I wanted to believe that about myself, but I felt defined by and stuck in my circumstances. I was trying to relate to God through a distorted lens based on what was happening in my life.

During this time when I was so lost in the story of my life and completely out of touch with myself, one of the most valuable things I did was spend time in nature. This, coupled with a lengthy consideration of the filters I was looking through, gave me an entirely new perspective on myself and thus a new existence.

Have you ever looked at a show-stopping sunset or a drop of dew on a blade of grass and sat inspired by the creation of beauty in front of you?

When I experience moments like this, the universe and its profound beauty is so overwhelming. It reaches deeply into my soul. Taking in the essence of the sunset or the pure, clean, crisp energy of the drop of dew on the grass requires no effort on my part. The exchange between this creation and my spirit simply happens. In that moment everything else around me may as well be frozen in time. I am part of the greatest whole that there is! I am part of the sunset, and it is part of me. The energy that composes me is of the same Source that composes the perfect sunset, night after night.

The difference between accepting my personal value and the soul-filling value of creation is that nothing blemishes the sunset. No one critiques sunsets! Nothing filters the magnificence of God in the sunset. It is overwhelming and obvious, day after day. It never loses its place in the order of the universe. It is always an astounding reminder of God.

As I spent time intentionally connecting to God in nature, the proof of my value became unmistakably apparent. I heard, "My dear one, *you* are that sunset! You are the droplet of dew on the perfectly cut blade of grass. You are a beam of sunshine bursting through a small opening in the clouds. You are the water in a fall crashing to the rock beneath. You are part of creation! You are connected to it. And it holds the truth of your core being. You, like the sunset, are a completely unique gift and design. You bring awareness and glory to God as people look on you and experience you as part of divine creation. This is the *truest* measure of your value."

When the lens of your self-perception is filled with faulty truths, it can be detrimental to your sense of self-worth. It is hard to treat yourself with kindness and respect when you don't feel worthy. It is easy to accept mistreatment. You are likely to make poor decisions. But when you align with your soul's worth and adjust your self-perception lens to match what is *really* the essence of who you are and how you deserve to be treated, everything changes.

In that moment at the window when I believed to the core of my being that I had tremendous value, I entered a journey of letting go of limitations and embracing freedom in my life! A heartfelt consideration of the filters that were clouding my ability to see value in myself, combined with *the truth of my created being and my connectedness to all of creation,* were the nuts and bolts of what allowed me to see myself through a different lens. From this knowledge of my worth I can more easily align with God and trust my judgement when I need to make an important decision.

The same is possible for you! I am hopeful that sharing a piece of my story will give you inspiration to begin RIGHT NOW knowing your value and loving yourself to pieces! It is your birthright.

I invite you to imagine what is possible in your life if you will align with God in the gift of your creation instead of unintentionally looking through the filters that are negating the truth of who you are and impacting your every decision and interaction. The practice of intentionally connecting to creation gave me the grounding I needed to remember my value and the courage to make good decisions and once again trust my gut.

The next time you find yourself overwhelmed with thoughts of self-abandonment and all the "shoulds" of a decision you are trying to make, I encourage you to take a moment to sit alone amid creation and find a connection to God and all the glory that is around and within you. Allowing that to be your guide, you *will* make decisions that honor who you are… and the entire world will be better for it!

Kara Stoltenberg, MA, Ed., works with individuals who have allowed themselves to be defined by others and the circumstances of their lives. Through online communities, live events, and individual work, Kara creates a safe, supportive environment for people to make tangible life changes. She empowers people to implement simple practices that have huge impact for change. If you're ready to remember your true value and make changes within a supportive community, join Kara at www.Karastoltenberg.com.

What Are You Waiting For? How Living My Purpose Saved My Life

Maria Stoumbos Styles

"There are lives only you can touch."
— *Harry Palmer, author of* The Avatar® *Course and the Avatar materials.*

THE DOCTORS WROTE ME OFF. Every couple of weeks my family met with the "experts" who tried to convince them to pull the plug. They argued, "Maria has a one percent chance of waking up to get stable enough for transplant." My dear loved ones always left the doctors with, "She hasn't told us what she wants to do, so NO!" They were having none of it.

Imagine living on life support for over four months in an infectious, long-term intensive care unit. Visiting hours were four times a day, and there were no chairs for visitors who were required to wear those sunny, yellow, paper hazmat suits and Barney-the-purple-dinosaur-colored latex gloves. My condition warranted such caution.

I was kept sedated in order to keep me stable, and was hooked up to tubes and machines that breathed for me and ran every major organ system. I blew up like a balloon, retaining fluids from complete inactivity. I lost all muscle tone, resulting in the loss of all mobility and function. My hands turned to claws; my feet got foot drop; my legs, arms, and neck became rubbery. I became a toxic, flattened, bloated pancake with rat's-nest hair and gorilla-length stubble. I was a sight!

Last rites were given regularly, but I hung in there. I didn't improve, but I was alive. My friends and family showed up like clockwork for weeks to watch over me and manage the overwhelming care of my body; to hold the space and process with me, watching and listening for responses through the beeps and dings my machines made. I was being supported so I could decide to stay or to go.

My body's decline was due to a rare lung disease called lymphangioleiomyomatosis, or LAM for short. My spiritual practice, Avatar, both practical and mystical, made it possible for me to work in consciousness even though the hospital staff couldn't fathom that I was even there anymore. But make no mistake; I was there and I was totally awake. I don't mean like the heart-wrenching, traumatized people on sedation who are helpless and feel the pain of the cuts of their surgical procedures as if they were awake. I'm talking about a state of awareness that transcends the body and the mind, being totally awake in consciousness even while under heavy sedation.

One day my family inspired a nurse to help them with a plan. They knew it was time. Four months had passed and I wasn't improving. They conspired to reduce the sedation that was keeping me stable, without a doctor's order. They wanted me to wake up and tell them what I wanted to do about my life.

They safely cut down my heavy sedation and I slowly woke up. I remembered nothing from the previous four months. I recognized that the hospital I was in was several hours away from the one where I had originally been hospitalized. A final lung collapse had precipitated the emergency treatment, tracheotomy, and medevac airlift to my LAM specialist hours away. I tried to ask the usual questions. That's when I noticed that there was a tube coming out of a hole in my throat, and that I had no voice. I got very curious. I tried to raise my arm to touch my throat, but it would only bend at the elbow, moving very slowly. I then saw my hand. It was a dry, flaky, claw-like appendage. (My fingers have never straightened out to this day.) I tried to move my arms, but I couldn't even adjust my pillow when my head slipped. I motioned for my family to pull back the covers. In shock, I saw the condition of my body.

I didn't have to wonder about my brain. There was some concern that I would have brain damage from loss of oxygen, but it was working perfectly. I knew this because I was furious at the condition of my body. After twelve years of dying from LAM – numerous lung collapses, surgeries, years of dragging oxygen tanks around, getting sicker and sicker until the last lung collapse landed me on life support – I realized that I was now further away from qualifying for a double lung transplant, the life-saving procedure that required that I have a functional body that could walk, talk, lift weights, and do cardio exercise in order to recover and use its new lungs! I was livid!

But I was alive. It was time to get busy and get the hell out of there. I knew in my heart that I had decided to stay and to do whatever it would take to get up, walk, qualify for transplant, recover, and get back to the work that I loved.

I'm an Avatar Master/Wizard, which means having the power, training, and support to help awaken people to who they really are and to watch them grow with the knowledge that they are not their bodies, or their minds, or anything else the world wants to use to define them. It means guiding them with the Avatar tools to realize that they are ineffable Source, undefinable, indestructible, and infinite, and that working together they can make the world better with no possibility of failure. It was what made it possible for me to screw up my courage, get my ass off that bed, and intend for the perfect set of lungs to arrive before it was too late. The doctors gave me six months to live – off life support. I took those odds and gave my first directive to the doctors: "Get me out of here!"

The lungs were a perfect match. The gift of life was offered by a grieving family who had just lost their nineteen-year-old boy, Joe Jr. I learned later that he saved many lives that day.

Now it was nearly a year after the day I had woken up on life support. My recovery, from the time of the transplant to getting back to work — took two years. I gradually made my way back to the work that had saved my life. I knew then, and continue to believe today, that helping others awaken is the purpose of my life; that only *how* you choose to help others remains to be explored, felt, committed to, and acted on; and that that action is what can save your life, figuratively and actually.

Avatar is the most powerful personal development program delivered at any price, by the kindest, least judgmental, most powerful, purposeful, and insistent-on-your-success group of people I've ever known. I thank God that I lived, because I simply wasn't done yet. And if you are reading this, you aren't done yet either. Knowing your purpose and finding the work you are meant to do to serve that purpose will save your life. Are you still searching for your purpose? Here's the good news: Trust that you are on your purpose the moment you open your eyes and breathe the air of this Earth. Stop looking and start walking. You are the vehicle for what you are here to contribute. Your life has meaning as you live it. Just decide to admit to yourself what excites you most. Decide what makes your life worth living. Decide what "juices" you and makes you feel buoyant and alive.

After surviving life support, recovering from a lung transplant, and getting back to my loved ones at home and my teammates in the global Avatar network, I was ready for the next stretch. I needed to tell my story to be able to reach more people who are ready to make a change and get on with what they are here for.

I am well, healthy, happy, and in love with my soul mate, fully recovered from an ordeal I wouldn't wish on my worst enemy. I'm in awe. I've looked inward a long time to overcome the "voice" so that I could emerge, authentically me, to sincerely help somebody. You know the voice – the one that likes to edit, judge, and discourage you.

It was time to tell my story after so many years of not fully showing up, not taking full responsibility for the evolution of the planet, and not doing my best. I had to stretch. Harry says, "Consciousness loves a stretch!" I was ready for the Transformational Author Experience and this group of amazing writers of which this book is the result. I discovered another worldwide network of spiritually awakening people who are doing what excites them. Each step, each decision, each word committed to paper, each person's journey as told by their heart transformed them personally, forever. As a teacher and an author, I believe that my purpose to help transform the world one person at a time expanded so that I could give myself permission to answer the call and touch even more lives. I needed to tell more people that they were right where they needed to be to get started on their journey of self-discovery; that if they looked around at the people in their lives they would see that these are their people, the ones only they can touch; that they didn't have to go far to start. What are you waiting for? Get started. Go out there and help someone.

Avatar®; ReSurfacing®; and Star's Edge, International® are registered trademarks of Star's Edge, Inc. All rights reserved.

⌒ↄ⌒

Maria Stoumbos Styles, teacher, writer, and speaker, celebrates the miracle of being alive by continuing her transformational work as an Avatar Master/Wizard. She delivers the Avatar Course worldwide with people committed to changing the world. Maria believes that who we are becoming and who we can serve is our purpose, and invites everyone to stop looking and start helping. If you are ready to serve the world, start with YOU! Visit www.AvatarHerenow.com for more information.

Become a Contributing Author
in the Next Wave of

Pebbles in the Pond:

Transforming the World One Person at a Time

IF YOU WANT TO SHARE YOUR STORY in the next "Wave" in this series, and believe in the powerful impact one voice (*your story*) can have on truly making a difference, I want to hear from you!

Ask any one of the authors in this series and they'll tell you that it's been a life-changing experience to be a contributing author to *Pebbles in the Pond.* Beyond the accomplishment of getting published alongside some of today's most successful authors, you'll become part of a powerful "mastermind family," or as we've come to call it — a MasterHeart.

You'll make valuable connections and lifelong friendships with like-minded authors. And you'll receive twelve months of guidance and coaching to help you share your story and get started as a Transformational Author.

If you're interested in applying to be a contributor in the next "Wave," please email Info@ChristineKloser.com right away to get more details.

I hope to have the opportunity to work with you and help you write and publish your transformational story.

Many blessings,

Christine Kloser
Spiritual Guide ~ Award-Winning Author
Transformational Book Coach
President, Transformation Books

Connect With Christine Kloser

Website
www.ChristineKloser.com

FREE Transformational Author Training
If you want help writing your *own* book, visit:
www.TransformationalAuthor.com or
www.GetYourBookDone.com/free-training

Got a Manuscript and Need Help with Publishing?
www.TransformationBooks.com

Social Media
www.Facebook.com/christinekloserfanpage
www.Facebook.com/transformationalauthors
www.twitter.com/christinekloser

Mail
Christine Kloser Companies LLC
211 Pauline Drive #513
York, PA 17402

Phone
(800) 930-3713

Email
Info@ChristineKloser.com

About Christine Kloser

Christine Kloser is a Spiritual Guide, Award-Winning Author, and Transformational Book Coach whose spot-on guidance transforms the lives of visionary entrepreneurs and authors around the world. Her passion is fueled by her own transformation in December of 2010 when, after much success as an entrepreneur, she found herself curled up in a ball on the floor sobbing because she had lost it all. When she let go of the last shred of stability and security in her life, she discovered her truth and the blessings began to flow.

From that place, she fearlessly (and faithfully) went on to create the most abundant, impactful, and joyous success of her life in a matter of a few short months as a pioneering leader of the Transformational Author movement. Christine knows how to flip the switch from "broke" to "blessed" and shares her wisdom through her books, award-winning email newsletter, and speaking and coaching programs.

She's been featured in the *Los Angeles Times, Entrepreneur Magazine, Atlanta Constitution-Journal, Leadership Excellence, FOX News,* Forbes.com, *Huffington Post,* and Entrepreneur.com, and is a regular columnist for the award-winning *PUBLISHED* Magazine. Her books and publications have received numerous awards including the Nautilus Book Silver Award, Pinnacle Book Award, National Best Books Award, and Apex Award for Publication Excellence.

Her greatest reward, however, is witnessing her clients as they step into their true power, tell their authentic stories, become published authors… and make their difference in the world.

After living in Los Angeles, California, for fourteen years, Christine now resides in York, Pennsylvania, with her husband, David, and daughter, Janet, where they enjoy a slower-paced, more relaxed lifestyle.

Learn more about Christine at www.ChristineKloser.com.